INDEPENDENT STUDY GUIDE

Microsoft DP-750 Exam Study Guide 2026

Azure Databricks Data Engineer Certification

✓ 120 practice questions with detailed explanations
✓ 13 chapters covering all exam domains
✓ Python and SQL code examples throughout

Meridian Certification Press
An imprint of Big Five Killer

Microsoft DP-750 Exam Study Guide 2026
Azure Databricks Data Engineer Certification

Published by Meridian Certification Press
An imprint of Big Five Killer

ISBN 978-1-60888-713-2 (Paperback)
ISBN 978-1-60888-714-9 (Hardcover)

AI Disclosure. Portions of this book were drafted with the assistance of large language models. All content was reviewed, edited, and verified by the editorial team at Meridian Certification Press. Practice questions and answer explanations underwent adversarial accuracy review.

Accuracy Commitment. If you believe you have found an error, please report it to `meridian@bigfivekiller.online`.

First edition, April 2026.

Contents

1 Chapter 1: About This Guide & Exam Overview **1**
1.1 Welcome to This Study Guide 1
1.1.1 Who This Guide Is For 1
1.1.2 How to Use This Guide 1
1.2 Exam Overview 2
1.2.1 Exam Format and Logistics 2
1.2.2 Exam Domains and Weightings 2
1.2.3 Detailed Exam Objectives 2
1.3 Study Strategies 3
1.3.1 The 4-Week Study Plan 3
1.3.2 Hands-On Practice 3
1.3.3 Key Documentation Resources 4
1.4 About Meridian Certification Press 4
1.4.1 Conventions Used in This Guide 4
1.5 Exam Day Preparation 4
1.5.1 Before the Exam 4
1.5.2 During the Exam 5
1.5.3 After the Exam 5
1.6 Chapter Summary 5
1.7 Practice Questions 5
1.8 Answer Explanations 5
1.9 Learning Objectives 6
1.10 Azure Databricks Architecture Overview 6
1.10.1 The Two-Plane Architecture 6
1.10.2 Key Architectural Components 7
1.11 Creating and Configuring Workspaces 7
1.11.1 Workspace Provisioning 7
1.11.2 Pricing Tiers 8
1.11.3 Workspace Configuration Settings 8
1.12 Cluster Management 8
1.12.1 Cluster Types 8
1.12.2 Cluster Configuration 9
1.12.3 Databricks Runtime Versions 9
1.12.4 Cluster Policies 10
1.12.5 Instance Pools 10
1.13 Workspace Organization Best Practices 11
1.13.1 Folder Structure 11
1.13.2 Git Integration (Repos) 11
1.13.3 Multiple Workspace Patterns 11
1.14 DBFS and Storage Integration 12
1.14.1 DBFS Overview 12
1.14.2 Mounting External Storage (Legacy) 12
1.14.3 Unity Catalog Volumes (Recommended) 12
1.15 The Databricks Utilities (dbutils) 12
1.15.1 File System Utilities 12
1.15.2 Widget Utilities 13
1.15.3 Secrets Utilities 13
1.15.4 Notebook Utilities 13
1.16 Chapter Summary 13
1.17 Practice Questions 14

1.18 Answer Explanations 14
1.19 Learning Objectives 15
1.20 Introduction to Unity Catalog 15
1.21 The Three-Level Namespace 15
1.21.1 Hierarchy Levels 16
1.21.2 Default Catalog and Schema 16
1.22 Metastore Configuration 17
1.22.1 Creating a Metastore 17
1.22.2 Managed Storage 17
1.22.3 Access Connectors 17
1.23 Storage Credentials and External Locations 18
1.23.1 Storage Credentials 18
1.23.2 External Locations 18
1.23.3 Storage Credential vs. External Location 18
1.24 Managed vs. External Tables 18
1.24.1 Managed Tables 18
1.24.2 External Tables 19
1.25 Access Control and Permissions 19
1.25.1 The Permission Model 19
1.25.2 Privilege Hierarchy 19
1.25.3 Ownership 20
1.25.4 Identity Federation 20
1.26 Volumes 20
1.26.1 Managed Volumes 20
1.26.2 External Volumes 21
1.26.3 Accessing Volume Files 21
1.27 Data Lineage 21
1.27.1 Table-Level Lineage 21
1.27.2 Column-Level Lineage 21
1.28 Delta Sharing 22
1.28.1 Sharing Data 22
1.28.2 Consuming Shared Data 22
1.29 Information Schema 22
1.30 Chapter Summary 23
1.31 Practice Questions 23
1.32 Answer Explanations 24
1.33 Learning Objectives 24
1.34 What Is Delta Lake? 25
1.34.1 Delta Lake vs. Raw Parquet 25
1.35 The Delta Transaction Log 25
1.35.1 How It Works 25
1.35.2 Checkpoints 26
1.35.3 ACID Guarantees 26
1.36 Creating Delta Tables 26
1.36.1 CREATE TABLE Syntax 26
1.36.2 CREATE TABLE AS SELECT (CTAS) 26
1.36.3 Creating Tables with PySpark 27
1.37 Reading and Writing Data 27
1.37.1 Reading Delta Tables 27
1.37.2 Writing to Delta Tables 27
1.38 DML Operations 28
1.38.1 UPDATE 28
1.38.2 DELETE 28
1.38.3 MERGE (Upsert) 28
1.39 Time Travel 29

1.39.1 Query by Version Number 29
1.39.2 Query by Timestamp 29
1.39.3 Table History 29
1.39.4 Restoring a Table 30
1.40 Table Optimization 30
1.40.1 OPTIMIZE (Compaction) 30
1.40.2 Z-ORDER 30
1.40.3 VACUUM 30
1.40.4 Liquid Clustering (Preview) 31
1.41 Schema Enforcement and Evolution 31
1.41.1 Schema Enforcement 31
1.41.2 Schema Evolution 31
1.42 Constraints and Generated Columns 32
1.42.1 CHECK Constraints 32
1.42.2 NOT NULL Constraints 32
1.42.3 Generated Columns 32
1.43 Table Properties 33
1.44 Chapter Summary 33
1.45 Practice Questions 33
1.46 Answer Explanations 34
1.47 Learning Objectives 35
1.48 The Medallion Architecture 35
1.48.1 Bronze Layer (Raw) 35
1.48.2 Silver Layer (Cleansed) 36
1.48.3 Gold Layer (Business-Level Aggregates) 37
1.48.4 Layer Comparison Summary 37
1.49 Catalog and Schema Organization 38
1.49.1 Environment-Based Organization 38
1.49.2 Domain-Based Organization 38
1.49.3 Hybrid Organization 38
1.50 Partitioning Strategies 39
1.50.1 Traditional Partitioning 39
1.50.2 Liquid Clustering (Recommended) 39
1.51 Slowly Changing Dimensions (SCD) 39
1.51.1 SCD Type 1 (Overwrite) 39
1.51.2 SCD Type 2 (Historical Tracking) 40
1.52 Data Quality Patterns 41
1.52.1 Quarantine Pattern 41
1.52.2 Expectation-Based Quality 42
1.53 Views and Materialized Views 42
1.53.1 Standard Views 42
1.53.2 Dynamic Views for Security 42
1.54 Chapter Summary 43
1.55 Practice Questions 43
1.56 Answer Explanations 44
1.57 Learning Objectives 44
1.58 Ingestion Overview 44
1.58.1 When to Use Each Approach 44
1.59 Auto Loader (cloudFiles) 45
1.59.1 Basic Auto Loader Configuration 45
1.59.2 Supported File Formats 45
1.59.3 CSV-Specific Configuration 46
1.59.4 JSON-Specific Configuration 46
1.60 Auto Loader File Discovery Modes 46
1.60.1 Directory Listing Mode (Default) 46

1.60.2 File Notification Mode 47
1.61 Schema Inference and Evolution 47
1.61.1 Schema Inference 47
1.61.2 Schema Evolution 47
1.61.3 The Rescued Data Column 48
1.61.4 Providing an Explicit Schema 48
1.62 Auto Loader Trigger Modes 48
1.62.1 Continuous Processing 49
1.62.2 Trigger Available Now 49
1.62.3 Trigger Once (Legacy) 49
1.63 COPY INTO 49
1.63.1 Basic COPY INTO Syntax 49
1.63.2 COPY INTO with CSV Files 50
1.63.3 COPY INTO with Pattern Matching 50
1.63.4 COPY INTO with Column Selection 50
1.63.5 Key COPY INTO Behaviors 50
1.64 Ingestion Metadata 51
1.64.1 Auto Loader Metadata 51
1.64.2 COPY INTO Metadata 51
1.65 Error Handling and Troubleshooting 51
1.65.1 Handling Corrupt Records 51
1.65.2 Parse Modes 52
1.65.3 Common Issues and Solutions 52
1.66 Auto Loader vs. COPY INTO Decision Matrix 52
1.67 Chapter Summary 53
1.68 Practice Questions 53
1.69 Answer Explanations 54
1.70 Learning Objectives 54
1.71 The Two APIs: Spark SQL and PySpark DataFrames 54
1.72 Reading Data 55
1.72.1 Reading from Tables 55
1.72.2 Reading from Files 55
1.72.3 Creating Temporary Views 55
1.73 Core Transformations 56
1.73.1 SELECT and Column Operations 56
1.73.2 Filtering (WHERE) 56
1.73.3 Sorting (ORDER BY) 57
1.73.4 Deduplication 57
1.74 Aggregations 58
1.74.1 Basic Aggregations 58
1.74.2 Multiple Grouping 58
1.75 Built-In Functions 59
1.75.1 String Functions 59
1.75.2 Date and Timestamp Functions 60
1.75.3 Conditional Functions 60
1.76 Working with Complex Types 61
1.76.1 Structs 61
1.76.2 Arrays 62
1.76.3 Maps 62
1.77 Type Conversions 63
1.78 Writing Transformed Data 64
1.79 Chapter Summary 64
1.80 Practice Questions 65
1.81 Answer Explanations 65
1.82 Learning Objectives 66

1.83 Join Operations 66
1.83.1 Inner Join 66
1.83.2 Left Outer Join 66
1.83.3 Right Outer Join 67
1.83.4 Full Outer Join 67
1.83.5 Cross Join 67
1.83.6 Left Semi Join 67
1.83.7 Left Anti Join 68
1.83.8 Join Column Handling 68
1.84 Broadcast Joins 68
1.85 Window Functions 69
1.85.1 Window Specification 69
1.85.2 Ranking Functions 69
1.85.3 Aggregate Window Functions 70
1.85.4 Offset Functions (LAG and LEAD) 71
1.85.5 Window Frame Specifications 72
1.86 Pivot and Unpivot 72
1.86.1 Pivot (Rows to Columns) 72
1.86.2 Unpivot (Columns to Rows) 73
1.87 User-Defined Functions (UDFs) 73
1.87.1 Python UDFs 73
1.87.2 Pandas UDFs (Vectorized UDFs) 74
1.87.3 SQL UDFs 74
1.87.4 UDF Performance Comparison 75
1.88 Higher-Order Functions 75
1.88.1 TRANSFORM 75
1.88.2 FILTER 75
1.88.3 AGGREGATE (REDUCE) 76
1.88.4 EXISTS and FORALL 76
1.89 Set Operations 76
1.90 Common Table Expressions (CTEs) 77
1.91 Chapter Summary 78
1.92 Practice Questions 78
1.93 Answer Explanations 79
1.94 Learning Objectives 79
1.95 Introduction to Structured Streaming 79
1.95.1 The Unbounded Table Model 80
1.95.2 Key Guarantees 80
1.96 Streaming Sources 80
1.96.1 Delta Lake as a Streaming Source 80
1.96.2 Auto Loader (Cloud Files) as Source 80
1.96.3 Apache Kafka as Source 81
1.96.4 Rate Source (Testing) 81
1.97 Streaming Sinks 81
1.97.1 Delta Lake Sink 81
1.97.2 Kafka Sink 81
1.97.3 Console Sink (Debugging) 82
1.97.4 Memory Sink (Testing) 82
1.98 Output Modes 82
1.98.1 Append Mode (Default) 82
1.98.2 Complete Mode 82
1.98.3 Update Mode 83
1.99 Trigger Modes 83
1.99.1 Default (Micro-Batch) 83
1.99.2 Fixed Interval 83

1.99.3 Available Now 84
1.99.4 Once (Legacy) 84
1.100 Watermarks and Late Data 84
1.100.1 The Late Data Problem 84
1.100.2 Defining Watermarks 84
1.101 Windowed Aggregations 85
1.101.1 Tumbling Windows (Non-Overlapping) 85
1.101.2 Sliding Windows (Overlapping) 86
1.101.3 Session Windows 86
1.102 Stream-Stream Joins 86
1.103 Checkpoints and Fault Tolerance 87
1.103.1 Checkpoint Location 87
1.103.2 Checkpoint Rules 87
1.104 Monitoring Streaming Queries 87
1.104.1 Query Progress 87
1.104.2 Key Metrics 88
1.104.3 Stopping a Stream 88
1.105 Change Data Feed (CDF) 88
1.106 Chapter Summary 89
1.107 Practice Questions 89
1.108 Answer Explanations 90
1.109 Learning Objectives 90
1.110 Introduction to Delta Live Tables 90
1.110.1 Why DLT? 91
1.110.2 Key Concepts 91
1.111 Creating DLT Datasets with Python 91
1.111.1 Materialized Views 91
1.111.2 Streaming Tables 92
1.111.3 Views (Intermediate Computations) 92
1.111.4 Reading from Other DLT Datasets 92
1.112 Creating DLT Datasets with SQL 93
1.112.1 Materialized Views in SQL 93
1.112.2 Streaming Tables in SQL 93
1.112.3 Views in SQL 93
1.112.4 Referencing DLT Datasets in SQL 93
1.113 Data Quality Expectations 94
1.113.1 Three Expectation Actions 94
1.113.2 Multiple Expectations 94
1.113.3 SQL Expectations 95
1.114 Complete Medallion Pipeline Example 95
1.114.1 Python Pipeline 95
1.114.2 SQL Pipeline 97
1.115 Pipeline Configuration 98
1.115.1 Pipeline Settings 98
1.115.2 Development vs. Production Mode 98
1.115.3 Continuous vs. Triggered Execution 99
1.115.4 Pipeline Parameters 99
1.116 The DLT Event Log 99
1.117 Advanced DLT Patterns 100
1.117.1 Apply Changes (CDC/SCD) 100
1.117.2 Parameterized Expectations 100
1.118 Chapter Summary 100
1.119 Practice Questions 101
1.120 Answer Explanations 101
1.121 Learning Objectives 102

1.122 Introduction to Databricks Workflows 102
1.122.1 Key Components 102
1.122.2 Task Dependencies 103
1.123 Creating Jobs 103
1.123.1 Using the UI 103
1.123.2 Using the Databricks CLI 103
1.123.3 Using the REST API 104
1.124 Task Types in Detail 105
1.124.1 Notebook Tasks 105
1.124.2 SQL Tasks 105
1.124.3 DLT Pipeline Tasks 105
1.124.4 Python Script Tasks 105
1.124.5 If/Else Condition Tasks 106
1.124.6 For Each Tasks 106
1.125 Job Scheduling 106
1.125.1 Cron-Based Scheduling 106
1.125.2 File Arrival Triggers 107
1.125.3 Continuous Jobs 107
1.126 Job Parameters and Task Values 107
1.126.1 Job Parameters 107
1.126.2 Task Values (Passing Data Between Tasks) 108
1.126.3 Dynamic Parameters 108
1.127 Error Handling and Retries 108
1.127.1 Task-Level Retries 108
1.127.2 Timeout Configuration 109
1.127.3 Conditional Failure Handling 109
1.127.4 Email Notifications 109
1.128 Compute Configuration 109
1.128.1 Job Clusters 109
1.128.2 Shared Job Clusters 110
1.128.3 Existing Clusters 110
1.128.4 Serverless Compute 110
1.129 CI/CD Integration 111
1.129.1 Databricks Asset Bundles (DABs) 111
1.130 Chapter Summary 111
1.131 Practice Questions 112
1.132 Answer Explanations 112
1.133 Learning Objectives 113
1.134 Monitoring Overview 113
1.135 Job Monitoring 113
1.135.1 Workflows UI 113
1.135.2 Run Status via API 114
1.135.3 Run Statuses 114
1.136 System Tables 114
1.136.1 Audit Logs 114
1.136.2 Billing and Usage 115
1.136.3 Table Lineage 115
1.136.4 Query History 115
1.137 Alerting 115
1.137.1 Job-Level Notifications 116
1.137.2 SQL Alerts 116
1.137.3 Data Quality Alerts 116
1.138 The Spark UI 117
1.138.1 Key Tabs 117
1.138.2 Reading the DAG Visualization 117

1.139 Common Performance Issues 117
1.139.1 Data Skew 118
1.139.2 Out of Memory (OOM) Errors 118
1.139.3 Small Files Problem 118
1.139.4 Shuffle Spill 119
1.140 Adaptive Query Execution (AQE) 119
1.140.1 AQE Features 119
1.140.2 How AQE Handles Skew 120
1.141 Troubleshooting DLT Pipelines 120
1.141.1 DLT Event Log Queries 120
1.141.2 Common DLT Issues 120
1.141.3 Full Refresh vs. Incremental Update 121
1.142 Logging Best Practices 121
1.142.1 Structured Logging in Notebooks 121
1.142.2 Custom Metrics with Task Values 121
1.142.3 Data Freshness Monitoring 122
1.143 Chapter Summary 122
1.144 Practice Questions 122
1.145 Answer Explanations 123
1.146 How to Use These Practice Exams 123

2 Practice Exam 1 **125**
2.1 Questions 125
2.2 Practice Exam 1—Answer Key 128

3 Practice Exam 2 **133**
3.1 Questions 133
3.2 Practice Exam 2—Answer Key 136

4 Practice Exam 3 **139**
4.1 Questions 139
4.2 Practice Exam 3—Answer Key 142
4.3 Scoring Guide 145
4.4 Final Study Tips 145

1

Chapter 1: About This Guide & Exam Overview

Meridian Certification Press—Microsoft DP-750: Implementing Azure Databricks Study Guide 2026

1.1 Welcome to This Study Guide

Welcome to the Meridian Certification Press study guide for the Microsoft DP-750: Implementing Azure Databricks certification exam. This guide has been designed to provide you with the comprehensive technical knowledge and hands-on understanding needed to pass the DP-750 exam and, more importantly, to become a proficient Azure Databricks practitioner.

The DP-750 exam validates your ability to implement, manage, and optimize data engineering solutions using Azure Databricks. As organizations increasingly adopt the lakehouse architecture to unify their data analytics and AI workloads, the demand for certified Databricks professionals continues to grow. This certification demonstrates your expertise in building production-grade data pipelines, implementing security best practices, and managing data governance through Unity Catalog.

1.1.1 Who This Guide Is For

This study guide is intended for:

- **Data engineers** preparing for the DP-750 certification exam
- **Database administrators** transitioning to cloud-based data platforms
- **Analytics engineers** who want to formalize their Databricks knowledge
- **Solutions architects** who design and implement lakehouse solutions on Azure

Prerequisites: Before attempting the DP-750 exam, you should have:

- At least 6 months of hands-on experience with Azure Databricks
- Working knowledge of Python and/or SQL
- Familiarity with cloud computing concepts, particularly on Microsoft Azure
- Understanding of basic data engineering concepts (ETL, data modeling, data warehousing)

1.1.2 How to Use This Guide

Each chapter in this guide follows a consistent structure:

1. **Learning objectives** aligned to specific exam domains
2. **Conceptual explanations** of key technologies and patterns
3. **Code examples** in PySpark and Spark SQL that you can run in your own Databricks workspace
4. **Exam tips** highlighted in callout blocks to help you focus on testable knowledge
5. **Practice questions** at the end of each chapter with detailed answer explanations

We recommend reading the chapters in order, as later chapters build on concepts introduced earlier. However, if you are already experienced in certain areas, you can use the exam domain mapping below to focus on your weakest areas.

1.2 Exam Overview

1.2.1 Exam Format and Logistics

The Microsoft DP-750: Implementing Azure Databricks exam consists of the following:

Attribute	Detail
Exam code	DP-750
Number of questions	40-60 questions
Question types	Multiple choice, multiple select, drag-and-drop, case studies
Duration	120 minutes
Passing score	700 out of 1000
Languages	English (additional languages may be available)
Registration	Microsoft Learn / Pearson VUE
Cost	$165 USD (subject to change)

The exam is proctored and can be taken at a Pearson VUE testing center or online with a remote proctor. You are not permitted to use external resources during the exam.

1.2.2 Exam Domains and Weightings

The DP-750 exam is organized into four major domains, each weighted according to its importance:

Domain	Weight	Chapters in This Guide
Domain 1: Implement and manage a lakehouse	25-30%	Chapters 2, 3, 4, 5
Domain 2: Transform data	25-30%	Chapters 6, 7, 8, 9, 10
Domain 3: Manage and monitor data pipelines	20-25%	Chapters 11, 12
Domain 4: Design and implement security	15-20%	Chapters 13, 14

> **Exam Tip:** Domains 1 and 2 together account for 50-60% of the exam. Make sure you are thoroughly comfortable with lakehouse implementation patterns and data transformation techniques before sitting the exam.

1.2.3 Detailed Exam Objectives

Domain 1: Implement and Manage a Lakehouse (25-30%)

- Configure and manage Azure Databricks workspaces
- Implement Unity Catalog for data governance
- Create and manage Delta Lake tables (managed and external)
- Implement medallion architecture (bronze, silver, gold)
- Manage schemas, catalogs, and volumes
- Configure metastore and storage credentials

Domain 2: Transform Data (25-30%)

- Read and write data using PySpark and Spark SQL
- Ingest data using Auto Loader and COPY INTO
- Perform data transformations including joins, aggregations, and window functions
- Implement user-defined functions (UDFs)
- Process streaming data using Structured Streaming
- Build and manage Delta Live Tables (DLT) pipelines
- Apply data quality constraints and expectations

Domain 3: Manage and Monitor Data Pipelines (20-25%)

- Create and schedule Databricks Workflows
- Monitor pipeline health and performance
- Implement alerting and notification strategies
- Troubleshoot pipeline failures
- Manage task dependencies and retry logic
- Implement CI/CD for data pipelines

Domain 4: Design and Implement Security (15-20%)

- Configure identity and access management (IAM)
- Implement network security (VNet injection, private endpoints)
- Apply row-level and column-level security
- Manage secrets using Azure Key Vault
- Configure data encryption at rest and in transit
- Implement audit logging and compliance

1.3 Study Strategies

1.3.1 The 4-Week Study Plan

For candidates with prior Databricks experience, we recommend the following study schedule:
Week 1: Foundations (Chapters 1-5) - Focus on workspace architecture, Unity Catalog, and Delta Lake - Set up a practice workspace in Azure if you do not already have one - Complete all practice questions for Chapters 2-5
Week 2: Data Transformations (Chapters 6-10) - Work through ingestion patterns, Spark transformations, and streaming - Run every code example in your practice workspace - Pay special attention to Delta Live Tables, which is heavily tested
Week 3: Operations and Security (Chapters 11-14) - Study pipeline orchestration, monitoring, and security - Practice creating Workflows with multi-task dependencies - Review IAM and network security configurations
Week 4: Review and Practice (Chapter 15 + Review) - Take the full practice exam in Chapter 15 - Review any topics where you scored below 80% - Re-read exam tips throughout the guide - Take 1-2 additional practice exams from online resources

1.3.2 Hands-On Practice

The single most effective study strategy for the DP-750 is hands-on practice. Microsoft provides a free Azure Databricks trial, and you can also use the Databricks Community Edition for many exercises. Throughout this guide, we provide code examples that you should type out and execute yourself rather than simply reading.

> **Exam Tip:** The DP-750 exam tests practical knowledge, not just theory. Many questions present code snippets and ask you to identify errors, predict outputs, or choose the correct approach. Hands-on experience is essential.

1.3.3 Key Documentation Resources

In addition to this study guide, we recommend bookmarking the following resources:

- **Microsoft Learn: Azure Databricks documentation**—The official Microsoft documentation is the primary source for exam content
- **Databricks documentation**—Provides detailed technical reference for all Databricks features
- **Databricks Academy**—Free courses that cover many exam topics
- **Delta Lake documentation**—Essential for understanding Delta Lake internals

---

1.4 About Meridian Certification Press

Meridian Certification Press specializes in producing high-quality certification study materials for cloud and data engineering professionals. Our guides are written by practitioners who hold the certifications they write about and who work with these technologies daily.

1.4.1 Conventions Used in This Guide

Throughout this guide, we use the following conventions:

- **Bold text** indicates key terms being defined for the first time
- `Monospace text` indicates code, commands, or configuration values
- Code blocks with syntax highlighting are used for multi-line code examples:

```python
# PySpark example
df = spark.read.format("delta").load("/mnt/data/sales")
df.show()
```

```sql
-- Spark SQL example
SELECT * FROM catalog.schema.sales_table LIMIT 10;
```

Special callout blocks are used for exam-relevant information:

> **Exam Tip:** These callouts highlight information that is particularly relevant to the exam. Pay close attention to these sections.

> **Warning:** These callouts highlight common mistakes or misconceptions that could lead to incorrect answers on the exam.

> **Note:** These callouts provide additional context or clarification that may help deepen your understanding.

1.5 Exam Day Preparation

1.5.1 Before the Exam

- Confirm your exam appointment at least 48 hours in advance
- Ensure your ID is current and matches your registration name
- If testing online, verify your system meets Pearson VUE requirements (webcam, microphone, stable internet)
- Get a good night's sleep—fatigue leads to careless mistakes

1.5.2 During the Exam

- Read each question carefully, including all answer options, before selecting
- Use the "Mark for Review" feature for questions you are unsure about
- Manage your time: aim to complete the first pass through all questions with at least 20 minutes remaining for review
- For code-based questions, trace through the logic step by step
- Eliminate obviously wrong answers first to improve your odds on uncertain questions

1.5.3 After the Exam

- You will receive your pass/fail result immediately upon completion
- A detailed score report will be available on your Microsoft Learn profile within 24 hours
- If you do not pass, review your score report to identify weak areas and focus your study accordingly
- You must wait 24 hours before retaking the exam

1.6 Chapter Summary

This chapter has provided you with:

- An overview of the DP-750 exam format, domains, and objectives
- A recommended 4-week study plan
- Guidance on how to use this study guide effectively
- Exam day tips and strategies

In the next chapter, we begin our technical deep dive with Azure Databricks architecture and workspace setup. Let us get started.

1.7 Practice Questions

Question 1: What is the passing score for the Microsoft DP-750 exam?

A. 650 out of 1000 B. 700 out of 1000 C. 750 out of 1000 D. 800 out of 1000

Question 2: Which exam domain has the highest weighting on the DP-750 exam?

A. Design and implement security B. Manage and monitor data pipelines C. Implement and manage a lakehouse (tied with Transform data) D. Only Transform data

Question 3: Which of the following is NOT a question type found on the DP-750 exam?

A. Multiple choice B. Case study C. Live coding lab D. Drag-and-drop

Question 4: How long do candidates have to complete the DP-750 exam?

A. 60 minutes B. 90 minutes C. 120 minutes D. 180 minutes

Question 5: Which study approach is MOST effective for preparing for the DP-750 exam?

A. Memorizing all Databricks API reference documentation B. Hands-on practice in a Databricks workspace combined with conceptual study C. Reading only the Microsoft Learn documentation D. Taking as many practice exams as possible without studying the underlying concepts

---

1.8 Answer Explanations

Question 1: B. The DP-750 passing score is 700 out of 1000. This is consistent with most Microsoft certification exams. Reference: Microsoft Learn exam registration page.

Question 2: C. Both "Implement and manage a lakehouse" and "Transform data" share the highest weighting at 25-30% each. Together they account for 50-60% of the exam. Reference: DP-750 exam skills outline.

Question 3: C. The DP-750 does not include live coding labs. Microsoft uses multiple choice, multiple select, drag-and-drop, and case study question formats. Some Microsoft exams include performance-based labs, but the DP-750 uses scenario-based questions instead. Reference: Pearson VUE exam format documentation.

Question 4: C. Candidates have 120 minutes (2 hours) to complete the DP-750 exam. Reference: DP-750 exam registration details.

Question 5: B. The most effective approach combines hands-on practice with conceptual study. The DP-750 tests practical knowledge through code-based scenarios, making hands-on experience essential. Simply memorizing documentation or taking practice exams without understanding the underlying concepts will not prepare you adequately. Reference: Microsoft certification preparation best practices. # Chapter 2: Azure Databricks Architecture and Workspace Setup

Meridian Certification Press—Microsoft DP-750: Implementing Azure Databricks Study Guide 2026

1.9 Learning Objectives

After completing this chapter, you will be able to:

- Describe the Azure Databricks architecture and its key components
- Explain the relationship between the control plane and data plane
- Create and configure Azure Databricks workspaces
- Manage clusters, including cluster policies and pools
- Understand the Databricks Runtime and its variants
- Configure workspace-level settings and access controls

1.10 Azure Databricks Architecture Overview

Azure Databricks is a first-party Microsoft Azure service built on the Apache Spark platform, developed in collaboration between Microsoft and Databricks. Understanding its architecture is fundamental to both the exam and real-world implementation.

1.10.1 The Two-Plane Architecture

Azure Databricks operates on a **two-plane architecture** that separates management functions from compute and data processing:

Control Plane (managed by Databricks): - Hosted in the Databricks cloud account - Manages the workspace UI, notebook service, and job scheduling - Stores notebook content, cluster configurations, and access control lists - Handles REST API requests and authentication - Manages the Unity Catalog metastore

Data Plane (runs in your Azure subscription): - Compute resources (VMs) run in your Azure subscription - Data remains in your Azure storage accounts (ADLS Gen2, Blob Storage) - Network traffic between workers stays within your VNet - You retain full control over data residency and network configuration

```
┌──────────────────────────────────────┐│

        Control Plane                 ││
   (Databricks-managed)              ││
                                      ││
 ┌───────────┐  ┌───────────────┐  ││
 │ Workspace │  │ Unity │Catalog ││
 │    UI     │  │  Metastore    │ ││
 └───────────┘  └───────────────┘  ││
 ┌───────────┐  ┌───────────────┐  ││
 │   REST    │  │     Job       │ ││
 │   API     │  │  Scheduler    │ ││
```

```
  └──────────┘  └──────────────┘  │ └────────────────┬────────────────┘

              │ Secure connection┌──────────────▼──────────────────┐│

          Data Plane                ││
   (Your Azure subscription)       ││
                                    ││
  ┌───────────────────────────┐    ││
  │   Databricks Clusters     │    ││
  │   (Driver + Workers)      │    ││
  └───────────────────────────┘    ││
                                    ││
  ┌───────────────────────────┐    ││
  │   Azure Storage           │    ││
  │   (ADLS Gen2 / Blob)      │    ││
  └───────────────────────────┘    │└──────────────────────────────────┘
```

Exam Tip: You must understand which components reside in the control plane versus the data plane. A common exam question asks where notebook code is stored (control plane) versus where the data being processed resides (data plane).

1.10.2 Key Architectural Components

Workspaces: A workspace is the primary organizational unit in Azure Databricks. It provides a collaborative environment where data engineers, data scientists, and analysts can work together. Each workspace is associated with: - A single Azure subscription - A single Azure region - One Unity Catalog metastore (for governance) - One or more Azure resource groups

Clusters: Clusters are sets of virtual machines that execute your workloads. They consist of: - A **driver node** that coordinates execution and maintains state - Zero or more **worker nodes** that perform distributed computation - A **Databricks Runtime** that provides the execution environment

Notebooks: Interactive documents that combine code (Python, SQL, Scala, R), visualizations, and narrative text. Notebooks execute against clusters.

Jobs: Scheduled or triggered executions of notebooks, JARs, Python scripts, or Delta Live Tables pipelines. Jobs can contain multiple tasks with dependencies.

DBFS (Databricks File System): A distributed file system abstraction mounted into each workspace. While DBFS is still supported, Unity Catalog volumes are the recommended approach for file management.

1.11 Creating and Configuring Workspaces

1.11.1 Workspace Provisioning

You can create an Azure Databricks workspace through multiple methods:

1. **Azure Portal**—GUI-based provisioning
2. **Azure CLI**—Command-line provisioning
3. **ARM/Bicep Templates**—Infrastructure as Code
4. **Terraform**—HashiCorp Infrastructure as Code

Here is an example using the Azure CLI:

```
# Create a resource group
az group create --name rg-databricks-prod --location eastus2

# Create a Databricks workspace (Premium tier for Unity Catalog)
az databricks workspace create \
  --resource-group rg-databricks-prod \
  --name dbw-analytics-prod \
  --location eastus2 \
```

```
  --sku premium \
  --managed-resource-group rg-databricks-managed
```

1.11.2 Pricing Tiers

Azure Databricks offers three pricing tiers:

Feature	Standard	Premium	Trial
Interactive notebooks	Yes	Yes	Yes
Job scheduling	Yes	Yes	Yes
Unity Catalog	No	**Yes**	Yes
Role-based access control	No	**Yes**	Yes
Audit logging	No	**Yes**	Yes
Conditional access / IP ACLs	No	**Yes**	Yes
Customer-managed keys	No	**Yes**	No

> **Exam Tip:** Unity Catalog requires the **Premium** pricing tier. If an exam question mentions Unity Catalog, data governance, or fine-grained access control, the workspace must be on the Premium tier. This is a frequently tested point.

1.11.3 Workspace Configuration Settings

After provisioning, several workspace-level settings should be configured:

Default Storage: Each workspace has a root DBFS storage location backed by an Azure Blob Storage account in the managed resource group. For production workloads, you should configure additional external storage using ADLS Gen2 with Unity Catalog external locations.

Network Configuration: By default, workspaces use a Databricks-managed VNet. For production deployments, you should configure: - **VNet injection**—Deploy the data plane into your own VNet - **Private Link**—Secure connectivity between the control plane and data plane - **No Public IP (NPIP)**—Clusters do not get public IP addresses

```
# Create workspace with VNet injection
az databricks workspace create \
  --resource-group rg-databricks-prod \
  --name dbw-analytics-prod \
  --location eastus2 \
  --sku premium \
  --vnet /subscriptions/{sub-id}/resourceGroups/{rg}/providers/Microsoft.Network/virtualNetworks/{vnet-
    name} \
  --private-subnet private-subnet-name \
  --public-subnet public-subnet-name \
  --no-public-ip
```

1.12 Cluster Management

1.12.1 Cluster Types

Azure Databricks supports several cluster types:

All-Purpose Clusters: - Interactive, shared clusters for development and ad-hoc analysis - Support multiple users and notebooks simultaneously - Can be started, stopped, and restarted manually - More expensive per DBU than job clusters

Job Clusters: - Created automatically when a job starts and terminated when it finishes - Dedicated to a single job run - Lower cost per DBU than all-purpose clusters - Cannot be used for interactive development

SQL Warehouses: - Optimized for SQL workloads (BI tools, dashboards) - Provide a SQL endpoint for JDBC/ODBC connectivity - Support serverless and classic deployment modes - Scale independently from Spark clusters

> **Exam Tip:** Know when to use each cluster type. Job clusters are preferred for production pipelines (lower cost, ephemeral). All-purpose clusters are for interactive development. SQL warehouses are for BI/analytics queries.

1.12.2 Cluster Configuration

When configuring a cluster, you specify several key parameters:

```python
# Example: Creating a cluster via the Databricks REST API
import requests
import json

cluster_config = {
    "cluster_name": "etl-production",
    "spark_version": "14.3.x-scala2.12",
    "node_type_id": "Standard_D4ds_v5",
    "num_workers": 4,
    "autoscale": {
        "min_workers": 2,
        "max_workers": 8
    },
    "spark_conf": {
        "spark.databricks.delta.preview.enabled": "true",
        "spark.sql.shuffle.partitions": "200"
    },
    "azure_attributes": {
        "first_on_demand": 1,
        "availability": "SPOT_WITH_FALLBACK_AZURE",
        "spot_bid_max_price": -1
    },
    "autotermination_minutes": 60,
    "data_security_mode": "USER_ISOLATION"
}
```

Key configuration options:

- **Spark version (Databricks Runtime):** Determines the Apache Spark version and included libraries
- **Node type:** The Azure VM size for driver and worker nodes
- **Autoscaling:** Dynamically adds or removes workers based on workload
- **Spot instances:** Use Azure Spot VMs for workers to reduce cost (up to 80% savings)
- **Auto-termination:** Automatically stops idle clusters after a specified period
- **Data security mode:** Controls how data access is governed (discussed in Chapter 13)

1.12.3 Databricks Runtime Versions

The Databricks Runtime (DBR) is the set of software components that runs on clusters. Key variants include:

Runtime	Description	Use Case
Databricks Runtime	Standard Apache Spark + Delta Lake + optimizations	General data engineering
Databricks Runtime ML	Standard + ML libraries (MLflow, TensorFlow, PyTorch)	Machine learning workloads

Runtime	Description	Use Case
Photon Runtime	C++ vectorized query engine for SQL/DataFrame workloads	High-performance SQL and ETL
Databricks Runtime for Genomics	Standard + genomics-specific libraries	Bioinformatics

> **Exam Tip:** The **Photon** runtime provides significant performance improvements for SQL and DataFrame workloads. It is the vectorized query engine built into Databricks that accelerates Delta Lake operations. Questions about performance optimization often reference Photon.

1.12.4 Cluster Policies

Cluster policies allow administrators to control cluster configurations by setting defaults and restrictions:

```
{
  "spark_version": {
    "type": "regex",
    "pattern": "14\\.[0-9]+\\.x-scala2\\.12",
    "defaultValue": "14.3.x-scala2.12"
  },
  "node_type_id": {
    "type": "allowlist",
    "values": [
      "Standard_D4ds_v5",
      "Standard_D8ds_v5",
      "Standard_D16ds_v5"
    ],
    "defaultValue": "Standard_D4ds_v5"
  },
  "autotermination_minutes": {
    "type": "range",
    "minValue": 10,
    "maxValue": 120,
    "defaultValue": 60
  },
  "num_workers": {
    "type": "range",
    "minValue": 1,
    "maxValue": 10
  }
}
```

Cluster policies help organizations: - **Control costs** by limiting VM sizes and maximum worker counts - **Enforce security** by requiring specific security modes or runtime versions - **Standardize configurations** across teams

1.12.5 Instance Pools

Instance pools maintain a set of idle, ready-to-use VM instances, reducing cluster start time from minutes to seconds:

- Pools keep a minimum number of instances ready (pre-warmed)
- When a cluster requests instances, they are drawn from the pool instantly
- Idle instances are automatically released after a configurable timeout
- Pools can use both on-demand and spot instances

```
# Pool configuration example
pool_config = {
    "instance_pool_name": "general-purpose-pool",
```

```
    "node_type_id": "Standard_D4ds_v5",
    "min_idle_instances": 2,
    "max_capacity": 20,
    "idle_instance_autotermination_minutes": 30,
    "azure_attributes": {
        "availability": "SPOT_WITH_FALLBACK_AZURE",
        "spot_bid_max_price": -1
    }
}
```

1.13 Workspace Organization Best Practices

1.13.1 Folder Structure

Organize your workspace with a clear, consistent folder hierarchy:

```
/Workspace├──
 /Repos                  # Git-integrated repositories│
   ├── /data-engineering  # Data pipeline code│
   └── /analytics         # Analysis notebooks├──
 /Shared                 # Shared notebooks and resources│
   ├── /Libraries         # Shared utility libraries│
   └── /Templates         # Notebook templates└──
 /Users                  # Per-user home directories
    ├── /user1@company.com
    └── /user2@company.com
```

1.13.2 Git Integration (Repos)

Databricks Repos provide native Git integration, enabling:

- Cloning repositories from GitHub, Azure DevOps, GitLab, and Bitbucket
- Branch management (create, switch, merge)
- Pull and push operations
- Code reviews through standard Git workflows

> **Exam Tip:** Databricks Repos is the recommended way to manage code in production. It enables CI/CD workflows and version control. Know that Repos syncs code from Git repositories into the workspace.

1.13.3 Multiple Workspace Patterns

For enterprise deployments, organizations typically use multiple workspaces to separate environments:

Pattern	Workspaces	Use Case
Environment separation	Dev, Staging, Prod	Standard SDLC
Regional separation	US-East, EU-West	Data residency compliance
Team separation	Engineering, Analytics, ML	Organizational isolation

Unity Catalog spans across workspaces within the same metastore, enabling consistent governance regardless of the workspace pattern chosen.

1.14 DBFS and Storage Integration

1.14.1 DBFS Overview

The Databricks File System (DBFS) is a distributed file system mounted into each workspace. It provides:

- A unified namespace for accessing data across different storage systems
- Integration with Azure Blob Storage and ADLS Gen2
- The `/mnt` directory for mounting external storage
- The `/FileStore` directory for serving files to web browsers

1.14.2 Mounting External Storage (Legacy)

While still supported, mount points are considered a legacy pattern. The recommended approach is to use Unity Catalog external locations and volumes.

```
# Legacy mount point (for reference only)
dbutils.fs.mount(
    source="wasbs://container@storageaccount.blob.core.windows.net/",
    mount_point="/mnt/data",
    extra_configs={
        "fs.azure.account.key.storageaccount.blob.core.windows.net":
            dbutils.secrets.get(scope="storage", key="access-key")
    }
)
```

1.14.3 Unity Catalog Volumes (Recommended)

Unity Catalog **volumes** provide governed access to files in cloud storage:

```
-- Create a managed volume
CREATE VOLUME my_catalog.my_schema.raw_files;

-- Create an external volume pointing to ADLS Gen2
CREATE EXTERNAL VOLUME my_catalog.my_schema.external_files
LOCATION 'abfss://container@storageaccount.dfs.core.windows.net/path';
```

```
# Access files through volumes
df = spark.read.csv("/Volumes/my_catalog/my_schema/raw_files/data.csv",
                    header=True, inferSchema=True)
```

> **Exam Tip:** For the DP-750 exam, Unity Catalog volumes are the preferred method for accessing files. Mount points using `dbutils.fs.mount()` are a legacy pattern. If a question asks for the "recommended" approach, choose volumes.

1.15 The Databricks Utilities (dbutils)

`dbutils` is a set of utility functions available in notebooks:

1.15.1 File System Utilities

```
# List files in a directory
dbutils.fs.ls("/Volumes/catalog/schema/volume/")
```

```
# Copy a file
dbutils.fs.cp("/source/path", "/dest/path")

# Move a file
dbutils.fs.mv("/source/path", "/dest/path")

# Remove a file or directory
dbutils.fs.rm("/path/to/remove", recurse=True)

# Display file head
dbutils.fs.head("/path/to/file.csv", maxBytes=1024)
```

1.15.2 Widget Utilities

```
# Create input widgets for parameterized notebooks
dbutils.widgets.text("start_date", "2026-01-01", "Start Date")
dbutils.widgets.dropdown("environment", "dev", ["dev", "staging", "prod"])

# Get widget values
start_date = dbutils.widgets.get("start_date")
env = dbutils.widgets.get("environment")
```

1.15.3 Secrets Utilities

```
# List available secret scopes
dbutils.secrets.listScopes()

# Get a secret value (never displayed in notebook output)
api_key = dbutils.secrets.get(scope="my-scope", key="api-key")
```

1.15.4 Notebook Utilities

```
# Run another notebook and get its result
result = dbutils.notebook.run("/path/to/notebook", timeout_seconds=300,
                              arguments={"param1": "value1"})

# Exit a notebook with a value
dbutils.notebook.exit("success")
```

> **Exam Tip:** Know the four categories of `dbutils`: `fs` (file system), `widgets` (parameterization), `secrets` (credential management), and `notebook` (orchestration). Questions often test which utility to use for a given task.

1.16 Chapter Summary

In this chapter, you learned:

- Azure Databricks uses a **two-plane architecture** separating the control plane (Databricks-managed) from the data plane (your Azure subscription)
- Workspaces require the **Premium tier** for Unity Catalog and advanced security features

- **Cluster types** serve different purposes: all-purpose for development, job clusters for production, SQL warehouses for analytics
- **Cluster policies** and **instance pools** help control costs and standardize configurations
- **Unity Catalog volumes** are the recommended replacement for DBFS mount points
- The **dbutils** module provides essential utilities for file operations, parameterization, secrets, and notebook orchestration

---

1.17 Practice Questions

Question 1: Which component of the Azure Databricks architecture manages notebook storage and the workspace UI?

A. Data plane B. Control plane C. Azure Storage account D. Managed resource group

Question 2: You need to create a Databricks workspace that supports Unity Catalog and role-based access control. Which pricing tier must you select?

A. Standard B. Premium C. Trial D. Basic

Question 3: A data engineer wants to reduce cluster startup time from 5 minutes to under 30 seconds. Which feature should they use?

A. Cluster policies B. Autoscaling C. Instance pools D. Spot instances

Question 4: Which cluster type is MOST cost-effective for running a nightly production ETL pipeline?

A. All-purpose cluster B. Job cluster C. SQL warehouse D. Serverless cluster

Question 5: What is the recommended approach for accessing files in cloud storage with Azure Databricks?

A. DBFS mount points using `dbutils.fs.mount()` B. Direct ABFSS paths with storage account keys C. Unity Catalog volumes D. Local file system paths

Question 6: A data engineer needs to parameterize a notebook so that it can be run with different date ranges. Which dbutils module should they use?

A. `dbutils.fs` B. `dbutils.widgets` C. `dbutils.secrets` D. `dbutils.notebook`

Question 7: Which Databricks Runtime variant includes a C++ vectorized query engine optimized for SQL and DataFrame workloads?

A. Databricks Runtime ML B. Databricks Runtime for Genomics C. Standard Databricks Runtime D. Photon Runtime

Question 8: Where do Databricks cluster compute resources (VMs) run in the Azure Databricks architecture?

A. In the Databricks control plane B. In your Azure subscription (data plane) C. In a shared Databricks compute pool D. In a dedicated Azure managed subscription

---

1.18 Answer Explanations

Question 1: B. The control plane, managed by Databricks, handles notebook storage, the workspace UI, REST API endpoints, and job scheduling. The data plane runs in your Azure subscription and handles compute and data processing. Reference: Azure Databricks architecture documentation.

Question 2: B. Unity Catalog, role-based access control, audit logging, and conditional access all require the Premium pricing tier. The Standard tier does not support these features. Reference: Azure Databricks pricing tier comparison.

Question 3: C. Instance pools maintain pre-warmed, idle VM instances that can be allocated to clusters almost instantly, reducing startup time from several minutes to seconds. Cluster policies control configurations but do not affect startup time. Reference: Databricks instance pools documentation.

Question 4: B. Job clusters are created when a job starts and terminated when it finishes. They have a lower DBU rate than all-purpose clusters and are the recommended choice for production pipelines. Reference: Databricks cluster types documentation.

Question 5: C. Unity Catalog volumes provide governed, secure access to files in cloud storage. Mount points are a legacy pattern, and direct storage account keys bypass governance. Reference: Unity Catalog volumes documentation.

Question 6: B. The `dbutils.widgets` module creates input widgets (text, dropdown, combobox, multiselect) that parameterize notebooks. Parameters can be set when running the notebook as a job. Reference: Databricks widgets documentation.

Question 7: D. Photon is the C++ vectorized query engine built into Databricks that accelerates SQL and DataFrame workloads. It provides significant performance improvements for Delta Lake operations. Reference: Databricks Photon documentation.

Question 8: B. Cluster VMs run in your Azure subscription (the data plane). This means your data never leaves your subscription, and you have full control over network and security configurations. Reference: Azure Databricks architecture overview. # Chapter 3: Unity Catalog and Data Governance

Meridian Certification Press—Microsoft DP-750: Implementing Azure Databricks Study Guide 2026

1.19 Learning Objectives

After completing this chapter, you will be able to:

- Explain the Unity Catalog architecture and its three-level namespace
- Configure metastores, catalogs, schemas, and tables
- Implement data governance using grants and permissions
- Manage external locations and storage credentials
- Apply data lineage tracking and auditing
- Differentiate between managed and external tables in Unity Catalog

---

1.20 Introduction to Unity Catalog

Unity Catalog is the unified governance solution for all data and AI assets on the Databricks Lakehouse Platform. It provides a single place to manage:

- **Data discovery**—Find and understand data assets across the organization
- **Access control**—Fine-grained permissions on tables, volumes, functions, and models
- **Auditing**—Track who accessed what data and when
- **Lineage**—Visualize data flow from source to consumption
- **Data sharing**—Securely share data across organizations using Delta Sharing

Before Unity Catalog, Databricks relied on workspace-level Hive metastores, which made cross-workspace governance difficult and inconsistent. Unity Catalog centralizes governance at the account level, spanning all workspaces attached to the same metastore.

> **Exam Tip:** Unity Catalog is a major focus of the DP-750 exam. Expect multiple questions about its namespace hierarchy, permission model, and configuration. Understand the difference between the old Hive metastore approach and Unity Catalog.

1.21 The Three-Level Namespace

Unity Catalog uses a **three-level namespace** to organize data assets:

```
catalog.schema.table
```

1.21.1 Hierarchy Levels

```
Account└──
 Metastore (one per region)
    ├── Catalog (logical container for schemas)
    │   ├── Schema (logical container for tables)
    │   │   ├── Table
    │   │   ├── View
    │   │   ├── Volume
    │   │   ├── Function
    │   │   └── Model
    │   └── Schema
    └── Catalog
```

Metastore: The top-level container for Unity Catalog. One metastore per Azure region, shared across all workspaces in that region. The metastore stores: - Metadata about all data assets - Access control policies - Audit logs - Lineage information

Catalog: A logical grouping of schemas. Common patterns include: - One catalog per environment (`dev`, `staging`, `prod`) - One catalog per business domain (`sales`, `marketing`, `finance`) - One catalog per team or department

Schema (Database): A logical grouping of tables, views, volumes, and functions within a catalog. Equivalent to a database in traditional RDBMS terminology.

```sql
-- Create a catalog
CREATE CATALOG IF NOT EXISTS analytics;

-- Create a schema within the catalog
CREATE SCHEMA IF NOT EXISTS analytics.sales;

-- Create a table with the full three-level name
CREATE TABLE analytics.sales.transactions (
    transaction_id BIGINT,
    customer_id BIGINT,
    amount DECIMAL(10,2),
    transaction_date DATE
);

-- Query using the three-level namespace
SELECT * FROM analytics.sales.transactions WHERE amount > 100;
```

1.21.2 Default Catalog and Schema

You can set default catalog and schema to avoid typing the full three-level name:

```sql
-- Set default catalog
USE CATALOG analytics;

-- Set default schema
USE SCHEMA sales;

-- Now you can reference tables by name alone
SELECT * FROM transactions WHERE amount > 100;
```

```python
# Set defaults in PySpark
spark.sql("USE CATALOG analytics")
spark.sql("USE SCHEMA sales")
df = spark.table("transactions")
```

Exam Tip: In exam questions, if a table reference includes all three levels (e.g., `catalog.schema.table`), it is using Unity Catalog. If it uses only a two-level reference (e.g., `database.table`), it may be using the legacy Hive metastore. The presence or absence of the catalog name is a key differentiator.

1.22 Metastore Configuration

1.22.1 Creating a Metastore

A Unity Catalog metastore is created at the Azure Databricks account level:

1. Navigate to the **Account Console** (accounts.azuredatabricks.net)
2. Go to **Data** > **Metastores**
3. Click **Create Metastore**
4. Provide:
   - Name (e.g., `metastore-eastus2`)
   - Region (must match workspace region)
   - ADLS Gen2 container for managed storage
   - Access connector (Azure managed identity)

1.22.2 Managed Storage

The metastore requires a **managed storage location** in ADLS Gen2 where managed tables and volumes store their data:

```
abfss://unity-catalog@storageaccount.dfs.core.windows.net/metastore-root
```

When you create a managed table, Delta Lake files are stored in this location automatically. You do not need to specify a path.

1.22.3 Access Connectors

An **Access Connector for Azure Databricks** is an Azure resource (managed identity) that Unity Catalog uses to access storage:

```
# Create an access connector
az databricks access-connector create \
  --resource-group rg-databricks \
  --name ac-databricks-uc \
  --location eastus2 \
  --identity-type SystemAssigned

# Grant Storage Blob Data Contributor role to the connector
az role assignment create \
  --assignee <connector-principal-id> \
  --role "Storage Blob Data Contributor" \
  --scope /subscriptions/{sub}/resourceGroups/{rg}/providers/Microsoft.Storage/storageAccounts/{sa}
```

Exam Tip: The Access Connector is the recommended way for Unity Catalog to authenticate with Azure Storage. It uses a managed identity, eliminating the need to manage storage account keys or SAS tokens. Know that the connector needs the **Storage Blob Data Contributor** role on the storage account.

1.23 Storage Credentials and External Locations

1.23.1 Storage Credentials

A **storage credential** encapsulates an authentication method for accessing external cloud storage:

```
-- Create a storage credential using an access connector
CREATE STORAGE CREDENTIAL IF NOT EXISTS adls_credential
WITH (
    AZURE_MANAGED_IDENTITY = (
        ACCESS_CONNECTOR_ID = '/subscriptions/{sub}/resourceGroups/{rg}/providers/Microsoft.Databricks
    /accessConnectors/ac-databricks-uc'
    )
);

-- Grant usage on the credential
GRANT CREATE EXTERNAL LOCATION ON STORAGE CREDENTIAL adls_credential TO `data-engineers`;
```

1.23.2 External Locations

An **external location** maps a cloud storage path to a storage credential, defining where external tables and volumes can be created:

```
-- Create an external location
CREATE EXTERNAL LOCATION IF NOT EXISTS raw_data_location
URL 'abfss://raw-data@storageaccount.dfs.core.windows.net/'
WITH (STORAGE CREDENTIAL adls_credential);

-- Grant permissions on the external location
GRANT CREATE EXTERNAL TABLE ON EXTERNAL LOCATION raw_data_location TO `data-engineers`;
GRANT READ FILES ON EXTERNAL LOCATION raw_data_location TO `data-analysts`;
```

1.23.3 Storage Credential vs. External Location

Concept	Purpose	Scope
Storage Credential	How to authenticate	Entire storage account or container
External Location	Where to access	Specific path within storage

```
Storage Credential (authentication)
    └── External Location 1 (abfss://container@sa/path1/)
    └── External Location 2 (abfss://container@sa/path2/)
    └── External Location 3 (abfss://other-container@sa/path3/)
```

1.24 Managed vs. External Tables

1.24.1 Managed Tables

Managed tables store both metadata and data within Unity Catalog's managed storage:

```
-- Create a managed table (no LOCATION clause)
CREATE TABLE analytics.sales.customers (
```

```
    customer_id BIGINT,
    name STRING,
    email STRING,
    created_at TIMESTAMP
);

-- Insert data
INSERT INTO analytics.sales.customers VALUES
    (1, 'Alice Johnson', 'alice@example.com', current_timestamp()),
    (2, 'Bob Smith', 'bob@example.com', current_timestamp());
```

Characteristics of managed tables: - Data is stored in the metastore's managed storage location - Dropping the table deletes both metadata AND data - Unity Catalog manages the full lifecycle - Simpler to manage—no need to specify storage paths

1.24.2 External Tables

External tables store metadata in Unity Catalog but data in a user-specified location:

```
-- Create an external table (with LOCATION clause)
CREATE TABLE analytics.sales.legacy_orders
LOCATION 'abfss://raw-data@storageaccount.dfs.core.windows.net/orders/'
AS SELECT * FROM legacy_source.orders;
```

Characteristics of external tables: - Data is stored at the specified external location - Dropping the table deletes metadata only – data files remain - Requires an external location and storage credential - Useful for data shared across multiple systems

> **Exam Tip:** The key difference: dropping a **managed table** deletes data; dropping an **external table** preserves data. This is one of the most commonly tested Unity Catalog concepts. Look for the `LOCATION` clause to identify external tables.

1.25 Access Control and Permissions

1.25.1 The Permission Model

Unity Catalog uses a **grant-based permission model** where privileges are explicitly granted to principals (users, groups, or service principals):

```
-- Grant permissions on a catalog
GRANT USE CATALOG ON CATALOG analytics TO `data-team`;

-- Grant permissions on a schema
GRANT USE SCHEMA ON SCHEMA analytics.sales TO `data-team`;
GRANT CREATE TABLE ON SCHEMA analytics.sales TO `data-engineers`;

-- Grant permissions on a table
GRANT SELECT ON TABLE analytics.sales.transactions TO `data-analysts`;
GRANT MODIFY ON TABLE analytics.sales.transactions TO `data-engineers`;

-- Grant all privileges
GRANT ALL PRIVILEGES ON SCHEMA analytics.sales TO `admin-team`;
```

1.25.2 Privilege Hierarchy

Privileges in Unity Catalog follow a hierarchical inheritance model:

Privilege	Description	Applicable To
`USE CATALOG`	Access a catalog	Catalog
`USE SCHEMA`	Access a schema	Schema
`CREATE SCHEMA`	Create schemas in a catalog	Catalog
`CREATE TABLE`	Create tables in a schema	Schema
`SELECT`	Read data from a table	Table, View
`MODIFY`	Insert, update, delete data	Table
`ALL PRIVILEGES`	All applicable privileges	Any securable

Important: To query a table, a user needs: 1. `USE CATALOG` on the catalog 2. `USE SCHEMA` on the schema 3. `SELECT` on the table

All three privileges are required. Missing any one will result in an access denied error.

```
-- Common mistake: granting SELECT without USE CATALOG/USE SCHEMA
-- This will NOT work for the user:
GRANT SELECT ON TABLE analytics.sales.transactions TO `reader`;

-- This WILL work:
GRANT USE CATALOG ON CATALOG analytics TO `reader`;
GRANT USE SCHEMA ON SCHEMA analytics.sales TO `reader`;
GRANT SELECT ON TABLE analytics.sales.transactions TO `reader`;
```

Exam Tip: Remember the three-step permission chain: `USE CATALOG` + `USE SCHEMA` + `SELECT`. Exam questions often present a scenario where a user has `SELECT` on a table but cannot query it. The answer is almost always that they are missing `USE CATALOG` or `USE SCHEMA`.

1.25.3 Ownership

Every securable object in Unity Catalog has an **owner**. The owner has all privileges on the object and can grant permissions to others:

```
-- Transfer ownership of a table
ALTER TABLE analytics.sales.transactions SET OWNER TO `data-engineering-lead`;

-- Transfer ownership of a schema
ALTER SCHEMA analytics.sales SET OWNER TO `data-team`;
```

1.25.4 Identity Federation

Unity Catalog integrates with Azure Active Directory (Microsoft Entra ID) for identity management:

- **Users** are synced from Entra ID via SCIM provisioning
- **Groups** from Entra ID can be used directly in Unity Catalog grants
- **Service principals** are used for automated pipelines and applications

---

1.26 Volumes

Unity Catalog **volumes** provide governed access to non-tabular files (CSVs, images, logs, model artifacts):

1.26.1 Managed Volumes

```sql
-- Create a managed volume
CREATE VOLUME analytics.sales.raw_files;

-- Upload files via the UI or CLI, then access:
SELECT * FROM csv.`/Volumes/analytics/sales/raw_files/data.csv`;
```

1.26.2 External Volumes

```sql
-- Create an external volume pointing to existing storage
CREATE EXTERNAL VOLUME analytics.sales.archive_files
LOCATION 'abfss://archive@storageaccount.dfs.core.windows.net/sales/';
```

1.26.3 Accessing Volume Files

```python
# Read files from a volume
import pandas as pd

# Using PySpark
df = spark.read.csv("/Volumes/analytics/sales/raw_files/data.csv",
                    header=True, inferSchema=True)

# Using Python (for small files)
pdf = pd.read_csv("/Volumes/analytics/sales/raw_files/data.csv")

# Write files to a volume
df.write.mode("overwrite").parquet("/Volumes/analytics/sales/raw_files/output.parquet")
```

1.27 Data Lineage

Unity Catalog automatically captures **data lineage**—the flow of data from source to destination:

1.27.1 Table-Level Lineage

Unity Catalog tracks: - Which tables were read to produce a given table (upstream lineage) - Which tables depend on a given table (downstream lineage) - Which notebooks, jobs, and pipelines interact with the data

1.27.2 Column-Level Lineage

Beyond table-level tracking, Unity Catalog captures column-level lineage: - Which source columns contributed to each target column - Transformation logic applied to columns - Helps with impact analysis when schema changes are planned

```sql
-- View lineage in SQL (through the Catalog Explorer UI)
-- Lineage is captured automatically when you run:
CREATE OR REPLACE TABLE analytics.sales.monthly_summary AS
SELECT
    date_trunc('month', transaction_date) AS month,
    SUM(amount) AS total_amount,
    COUNT(*) AS transaction_count
FROM analytics.sales.transactions
GROUP BY 1;
-- Unity Catalog automatically records that monthly_summary
```

```
-- depends on transactions.transaction_date and transactions.amount
```

Exam Tip: Lineage in Unity Catalog is captured **automatically**—no additional configuration is needed. It works across notebooks, jobs, and DLT pipelines. Know that lineage tracks both table-level and column-level dependencies.

1.28 Delta Sharing

Delta Sharing is an open protocol for secure data sharing, integrated into Unity Catalog:

1.28.1 Sharing Data

```
-- Create a share
CREATE SHARE IF NOT EXISTS sales_share;

-- Add tables to the share
ALTER SHARE sales_share ADD TABLE analytics.sales.transactions;
ALTER SHARE sales_share ADD TABLE analytics.sales.customers;

-- Create a recipient
CREATE RECIPIENT IF NOT EXISTS partner_analytics
USING ID 'partner-sharing-id';

-- Grant the share to the recipient
GRANT SELECT ON SHARE sales_share TO RECIPIENT partner_analytics;
```

1.28.2 Consuming Shared Data

```
-- Create a catalog from a share (as the recipient)
CREATE CATALOG IF NOT EXISTS partner_data
USING SHARE provider_name.sales_share;

-- Query shared data like any other table
SELECT * FROM partner_data.default.transactions;
```

1.29 Information Schema

Unity Catalog provides an **information schema** for programmatic discovery of metadata:

```
-- List all catalogs
SELECT * FROM system.information_schema.catalogs;

-- List all schemas in a catalog
SELECT * FROM analytics.information_schema.schemata;

-- List all tables in a schema
SELECT * FROM analytics.information_schema.tables
WHERE table_schema = 'sales';
```

```
-- List all columns in a table
SELECT * FROM analytics.information_schema.columns
WHERE table_schema = 'sales' AND table_name = 'transactions';

-- List all grants on a table
SELECT * FROM analytics.information_schema.table_privileges
WHERE table_schema = 'sales' AND table_name = 'transactions';
```

> **Exam Tip:** The `system.information_schema` catalog is the programmatic way to discover Unity Catalog metadata. Know that it contains views for catalogs, schemas, tables, columns, and privileges.

1.30 Chapter Summary

In this chapter, you learned:

- Unity Catalog provides **centralized governance** across all workspaces attached to a metastore
- The **three-level namespace** is `catalog.schema.table`
- **Metastores** are regional and require managed storage (ADLS Gen2) and access connectors
- **Storage credentials** handle authentication; **external locations** define accessible paths
- **Managed tables** store data in metastore storage (dropped = data deleted); **external tables** use user-specified storage (dropped = data preserved)
- Permissions follow a **grant-based model** requiring `USE CATALOG` + `USE SCHEMA` + object-level grants
- **Lineage** is captured automatically at both table and column levels
- **Delta Sharing** enables secure cross-organization data sharing
- **Volumes** provide governed access to non-tabular files

1.31 Practice Questions

Question 1: What is the correct three-level namespace format in Unity Catalog?

A. `schema.database.table` B. `metastore.catalog.table` C. `catalog.schema.table` D. `workspace.database.table`

Question 2: A data analyst has been granted `SELECT` on a table but receives an "access denied" error when querying it. What is the MOST likely cause?

A. The table does not exist B. The analyst is missing `USE CATALOG` and/or `USE SCHEMA` permissions C. The analyst does not have `MODIFY` permission D. The table is an external table

Question 3: What happens when you drop a managed table in Unity Catalog?

A. Only the metadata is deleted; data files remain B. Both metadata and data files are deleted C. The table is marked as inactive but data is retained for 30 days D. An error occurs because managed tables cannot be dropped

Question 4: Which Azure resource does Unity Catalog use to authenticate with ADLS Gen2 storage?

A. Storage account access key B. SAS token C. Access Connector with managed identity D. Azure Active Directory application registration

Question 5: A data engineer needs to share data with an external partner securely. Which Unity Catalog feature should they use?

A. External locations B. Delta Sharing C. Storage credentials D. Volumes

Question 6: How is data lineage captured in Unity Catalog?

A. Users must manually define lineage relationships B. Lineage is captured automatically when queries execute C. Lineage requires a separate Azure service to be configured D. Lineage is only available for DLT pipelines

Question 7: What is the purpose of an external location in Unity Catalog?

A. To store managed table data outside of the metastore B. To map a cloud storage path to a storage credential for governed access C. To create a connection to an external database like SQL Server D. To define a network endpoint for private connectivity

Question 8: Which information schema view would you query to find all columns in a specific table?

A. `system.information_schema.tables` B. `system.information_schema.schemata` C. `system.information_schema.columns` D. `system.information_schema.table_privileges`

Question 9: You need to provide governed access to CSV files stored in ADLS Gen2. What is the recommended Unity Catalog approach?

A. Create a DBFS mount point B. Create a Unity Catalog volume C. Copy the files to a managed table D. Use direct ABFSS paths with a storage account key

Question 10: How many metastores can be associated with a single Azure region?

A. One per workspace B. One per Azure subscription C. One per region (shared across workspaces) D. Unlimited

---

1.32 Answer Explanations

Question 1: C. The Unity Catalog three-level namespace is `catalog.schema.table`. The metastore sits above the catalog level but is not part of the table reference. Reference: Unity Catalog namespace documentation.

Question 2: B. To query a table, a user needs `USE CATALOG` on the catalog, `USE SCHEMA` on the schema, AND `SELECT` on the table. Missing any of these will result in access denied. Reference: Unity Catalog privilege model.

Question 3: B. Dropping a managed table deletes both metadata and the underlying data files. This is the key distinction from external tables, where only metadata is removed. Reference: Unity Catalog managed tables documentation.

Question 4: C. Unity Catalog uses Access Connectors for Azure Databricks, which leverage managed identities to authenticate with ADLS Gen2. This eliminates the need for storage keys or SAS tokens. Reference: Unity Catalog storage credential configuration.

Question 5: B. Delta Sharing is the Unity Catalog feature for securely sharing data with external partners. It uses an open protocol that allows recipients to access shared data without needing a Databricks workspace. Reference: Delta Sharing documentation.

Question 6: B. Unity Catalog automatically captures lineage when queries execute. No manual configuration is needed. Lineage works across notebooks, jobs, and DLT pipelines at both table and column levels. Reference: Unity Catalog lineage documentation.

Question 7: B. An external location maps a cloud storage path to a storage credential, defining where external tables and volumes can be created with governed access. Reference: Unity Catalog external locations documentation.

Question 8: C. The `system.information_schema.columns` view contains metadata about all columns in all tables. You can filter by `table_schema` and `table_name` to find columns for a specific table. Reference: Unity Catalog information schema documentation.

Question 9: B. Unity Catalog volumes provide governed access to non-tabular files including CSVs. Volumes support permissions, lineage, and auditing. DBFS mounts are a legacy pattern. Reference: Unity Catalog volumes documentation.

Question 10: C. There is one metastore per Azure region, and all workspaces in that region can be attached to the same metastore. This enables cross-workspace governance. Reference: Unity Catalog metastore documentation. # Chapter 4: Delta Lake Fundamentals

Meridian Certification Press—Microsoft DP-750: Implementing Azure Databricks Study Guide 2026

1.33 Learning Objectives

After completing this chapter, you will be able to:

- Explain the Delta Lake storage format and its advantages over raw Parquet
- Create, read, update, and delete data in Delta tables
- Use time travel to query historical versions of data
- Optimize Delta tables using OPTIMIZE, VACUUM, and Z-ORDER
- Understand the Delta Lake transaction log and ACID guarantees

- Work with table properties, constraints, and generated columns

---

1.34 What Is Delta Lake?

Delta Lake is an open-source storage layer that brings ACID transactions and reliability to data lakes. It sits on top of Apache Parquet files and adds a transaction log that enables:

- **ACID transactions**—Atomic, Consistent, Isolated, Durable operations
- **Scalable metadata handling**—Transaction log instead of file listing
- **Time travel**—Query previous versions of data
- **Schema enforcement**—Prevent bad data from corrupting tables
- **Schema evolution**—Safely add columns over time
- **Unified batch and streaming**—Same table for both workloads
- **DML operations**—UPDATE, DELETE, MERGE support on data lakes

Delta Lake is the default table format in Azure Databricks. When you create a table without specifying a format, it is created as a Delta table.

1.34.1 Delta Lake vs. Raw Parquet

Feature	Raw Parquet	Delta Lake
ACID transactions	No	**Yes**
UPDATE/DELETE/MERGE	No	**Yes**
Time travel	No	**Yes**
Schema enforcement	No	**Yes**
Concurrent reads/writes	Unsafe	**Safe**
Streaming support	Limited	**Full**
File compaction	Manual	**OPTIMIZE**

Exam Tip: Delta Lake is the foundation of the Databricks Lakehouse. Every content chapter in this guide builds on Delta Lake concepts. The exam heavily tests Delta Lake operations, time travel, optimization, and transaction log behavior.

1.35 The Delta Transaction Log

1.35.1 How It Works

Every Delta table has a `_delta_log` directory that contains an ordered sequence of JSON files (commit logs):

```
/delta-table/├──
 _delta_log/│
   ├── 00000000000000000000.json   # Version 0 (initial creation)│
   ├── 00000000000000000001.json   # Version 1 (first update)│
   ├── 00000000000000000002.json   # Version 2 (second update)│
   └── 00000000000000000010.checkpoint.parquet  # Checkpoint every 10 commits├──
 part-00000-xxx.snappy.parquet   # Data files├──
 part-00001-xxx.snappy.parquet└──
 part-00002-xxx.snappy.parquet
```

Each commit log entry records: - **Add file actions**—New data files added - **Remove file actions**—Old data files logically removed - **Metadata changes**—Schema changes, table properties - **Protocol changes**—Reader/writer version requirements

1.35.2 Checkpoints

Every 10 commits, Delta Lake creates a **checkpoint file** in Parquet format that consolidates the state of the transaction log. This prevents readers from needing to replay all individual commits:

```
Version 0: Read commit 0
Version 5: Read commits 0, 1, 2, 3, 4, 5
Version 12: Read checkpoint at 10, then commits 11, 12
Version 25: Read checkpoint at 20, then commits 21, 22, 23, 24, 25
```

> **Exam Tip:** Checkpoints are created every 10 commits by default. This is a frequently tested fact. The checkpoint reduces the number of JSON files that must be read to determine the current state of the table.

1.35.3 ACID Guarantees

Delta Lake provides full ACID guarantees:

- **Atomicity:** Each commit either fully succeeds or fully fails. Partial writes never corrupt the table.
- **Consistency:** Schema enforcement ensures data matches the expected structure.
- **Isolation:** Concurrent readers and writers operate without conflict using optimistic concurrency control.
- **Durability:** Once a commit is written to the transaction log, it is permanent.

1.36 Creating Delta Tables

1.36.1 CREATE TABLE Syntax

```
-- Create a managed Delta table
CREATE TABLE analytics.sales.orders (
    order_id BIGINT NOT NULL,
    customer_id BIGINT,
    product_name STRING,
    quantity INT,
    unit_price DECIMAL(10,2),
    order_date DATE,
    status STRING
)
USING DELTA
COMMENT 'Customer orders table'
TBLPROPERTIES (
    'delta.autoOptimize.optimizeWrite' = 'true',
    'delta.autoOptimize.autoCompact' = 'true'
);
```

1.36.2 CREATE TABLE AS SELECT (CTAS)

```
-- Create a table from a query
CREATE TABLE analytics.sales.high_value_orders AS
SELECT *
FROM analytics.sales.orders
WHERE unit_price * quantity > 1000;
```

1.36.3 Creating Tables with PySpark

```
from pyspark.sql.types import *

schema = StructType([
    StructField("order_id", LongType(), False),
    StructField("customer_id", LongType(), True),
    StructField("product_name", StringType(), True),
    StructField("quantity", IntegerType(), True),
    StructField("unit_price", DecimalType(10, 2), True),
    StructField("order_date", DateType(), True),
    StructField("status", StringType(), True)
])

# Create an empty Delta table
empty_df = spark.createDataFrame([], schema)
empty_df.write.format("delta").saveAsTable("analytics.sales.orders")

# Create from existing data
df = spark.read.csv("/Volumes/analytics/sales/raw/orders.csv",
                     header=True, schema=schema)
df.write.format("delta").saveAsTable("analytics.sales.orders")
```

1.37 Reading and Writing Data

1.37.1 Reading Delta Tables

```
# Read using table name (Unity Catalog)
df = spark.table("analytics.sales.orders")

# Read using Delta format with path
df = spark.read.format("delta").load("/path/to/delta-table")

# Read with SQL
spark.sql("SELECT * FROM analytics.sales.orders WHERE status = 'shipped'")
```

```
-- SQL queries
SELECT product_name, SUM(quantity) as total_qty
FROM analytics.sales.orders
WHERE order_date >= '2026-01-01'
GROUP BY product_name
ORDER BY total_qty DESC;
```

1.37.2 Writing to Delta Tables

```
# Append data
new_orders.write.format("delta").mode("append").saveAsTable("analytics.sales.orders")

# Overwrite data
daily_summary.write.format("delta").mode("overwrite").saveAsTable("analytics.sales.daily_summary")

# Insert with SQL
spark.sql("""
```

```
    INSERT INTO analytics.sales.orders VALUES
    (1001, 42, 'Widget Pro', 5, 29.99, '2026-03-01', 'pending')
""")
```

> **Exam Tip:** Know the four write modes: `append` (add rows), `overwrite` (replace all data), `ignore` (skip if table exists), `error/errorifexists` (fail if table exists, the default). The exam often presents scenarios asking which mode to use.

1.38 DML Operations

1.38.1 UPDATE

```sql
-- Update order status
UPDATE analytics.sales.orders
SET status = 'shipped', updated_at = current_timestamp()
WHERE order_id = 1001;

-- Conditional update
UPDATE analytics.sales.orders
SET unit_price = unit_price * 1.1
WHERE product_name = 'Widget Pro' AND status = 'pending';
```

1.38.2 DELETE

```sql
-- Delete specific records
DELETE FROM analytics.sales.orders
WHERE status = 'cancelled' AND order_date < '2025-01-01';

-- Delete with subquery
DELETE FROM analytics.sales.orders
WHERE customer_id IN (
    SELECT customer_id FROM analytics.sales.blocked_customers
);
```

1.38.3 MERGE (Upsert)

The `MERGE` statement is one of the most important Delta Lake operations, enabling upsert (insert or update) logic:

```sql
MERGE INTO analytics.sales.orders AS target
USING staging.sales.new_orders AS source
ON target.order_id = source.order_id
WHEN MATCHED AND source.status = 'cancelled' THEN
    DELETE
WHEN MATCHED THEN
    UPDATE SET
        target.status = source.status,
        target.quantity = source.quantity,
        target.unit_price = source.unit_price
WHEN NOT MATCHED THEN
    INSERT (order_id, customer_id, product_name, quantity, unit_price, order_date, status)
    VALUES (source.order_id, source.customer_id, source.product_name,
            source.quantity, source.unit_price, source.order_date, source.status);
```

```
# MERGE with PySpark (DeltaTable API)
from delta.tables import DeltaTable

target = DeltaTable.forName(spark, "analytics.sales.orders")

target.alias("t").merge(
    source_df.alias("s"),
    "t.order_id = s.order_id"
).whenMatchedUpdate(
    set={
        "status": "s.status",
        "quantity": "s.quantity",
        "unit_price": "s.unit_price"
    }
).whenNotMatchedInsertAll(
).execute()
```

Exam Tip: MERGE is extensively tested on the DP-750. Make sure you understand the three clauses: `WHEN MATCHED ... UPDATE`, `WHEN MATCHED ... DELETE`, and `WHEN NOT MATCHED ... INSERT`. Know that you can have multiple `WHEN MATCHED` clauses with different conditions.

1.39 Time Travel

Delta Lake retains the history of all changes, allowing you to query previous versions of a table.

1.39.1 Query by Version Number

```
-- Query a specific version
SELECT * FROM analytics.sales.orders VERSION AS OF 5;

-- Query the previous version
SELECT * FROM analytics.sales.orders VERSION AS OF
    (SELECT max(version) - 1 FROM (DESCRIBE HISTORY analytics.sales.orders));
```

```
# PySpark time travel
df_v5 = spark.read.format("delta").option("versionAsOf", 5).table("analytics.sales.orders")
```

1.39.2 Query by Timestamp

```
-- Query as of a specific timestamp
SELECT * FROM analytics.sales.orders TIMESTAMP AS OF '2026-03-01T12:00:00Z';
```

```
df_historical = (spark.read.format("delta")
    .option("timestampAsOf", "2026-03-01T12:00:00Z")
    .table("analytics.sales.orders"))
```

1.39.3 Table History

```
-- View the full history of a table
DESCRIBE HISTORY analytics.sales.orders;
```

Output includes: - Version number - Timestamp - Operation (WRITE, UPDATE, DELETE, MERGE, etc.) - User who performed the operation - Operation parameters - Number of rows affected

1.39.4 Restoring a Table

```
-- Restore a table to a previous version
RESTORE TABLE analytics.sales.orders TO VERSION AS OF 5;

-- Restore to a timestamp
RESTORE TABLE analytics.sales.orders TO TIMESTAMP AS OF '2026-03-01T12:00:00Z';
```

> **Exam Tip:** Time travel data is only available as long as the underlying data files exist. The `VACUUM` command (covered next) removes old data files. After VACUUM, time travel to versions older than the retention period will fail.

1.40 Table Optimization

1.40.1 OPTIMIZE (Compaction)

Small files degrade read performance. The `OPTIMIZE` command compacts small files into larger ones:

```
-- Optimize a table (compact small files)
OPTIMIZE analytics.sales.orders;

-- Optimize with Z-ORDER on frequently filtered columns
OPTIMIZE analytics.sales.orders
ZORDER BY (customer_id, order_date);
```

How OPTIMIZE works: 1. Identifies bins of small files (< target file size) 2. Rewrites each bin into one or more larger files (target: ~1 GB) 3. Updates the transaction log atomically 4. Old files are logically removed (but not physically deleted until VACUUM)

1.40.2 Z-ORDER

Z-ORDER reorganizes data within files to co-locate related values, dramatically improving query performance for filtered reads:

```
-- Z-ORDER on frequently filtered columns
OPTIMIZE analytics.sales.orders ZORDER BY (order_date, customer_id);
```

Z-ORDER works by: - Interleaving the sort order of specified columns using a Z-curve - Co-locating records with similar values in the same files - Enabling data skipping to eliminate files during queries

> **Exam Tip:** Z-ORDER is most effective on columns with **high cardinality** that are **frequently used in WHERE clauses.** Do not Z-ORDER on low-cardinality columns (like boolean or status fields) or columns rarely filtered on. Limit Z-ORDER to 2-4 columns for best results.

1.40.3 VACUUM

`VACUUM` physically deletes old data files that are no longer referenced by the transaction log:

```
-- Remove files older than 7 days (default retention)
VACUUM analytics.sales.orders;

-- Remove files older than a specific retention period
```

```
VACUUM analytics.sales.orders RETAIN 168 HOURS;

-- Dry run (preview what would be deleted)
VACUUM analytics.sales.orders DRY RUN;
```

Important considerations: - Default retention period is **7 days** (168 hours) - After VACUUM, time travel to versions older than the retention period will fail - VACUUM does NOT affect the transaction log—only data files - Setting retention below 7 days requires: `spark.databricks.delta.retentionDurationCheck.enabled = false`

> **Warning:** Never set VACUUM retention below 7 days in production without understanding the consequences. Concurrent readers may fail if their referenced files are deleted during a read operation.

1.40.4 Liquid Clustering (Preview)

Liquid Clustering is a newer optimization that replaces both Z-ORDER and partitioning:

```
-- Create a table with liquid clustering
CREATE TABLE analytics.sales.orders_lc (
    order_id BIGINT,
    customer_id BIGINT,
    order_date DATE,
    amount DECIMAL(10,2)
)
CLUSTER BY (order_date, customer_id);

-- Trigger clustering
OPTIMIZE analytics.sales.orders_lc;
```

Liquid clustering advantages: - Incrementally clusters data (no full rewrite) - Adapts to changing query patterns - Eliminates the need for partitioning decisions upfront - Works with OPTIMIZE command

---

1.41 Schema Enforcement and Evolution

1.41.1 Schema Enforcement

Delta Lake enforces schema on write by default. If incoming data does not match the table schema, the write fails:

```
# This will fail if new_data has extra or missing columns
new_data.write.format("delta").mode("append").saveAsTable("analytics.sales.orders")
# AnalysisException: A schema mismatch detected when writing to the Delta table.
```

1.41.2 Schema Evolution

You can enable schema evolution to allow the table schema to change automatically:

```
# Enable schema evolution for a specific write
new_data.write.format("delta") \
    .option("mergeSchema", "true") \
    .mode("append") \
    .saveAsTable("analytics.sales.orders")
```

```
-- Enable automatic schema evolution at the table level
ALTER TABLE analytics.sales.orders SET TBLPROPERTIES (
    'delta.columnMapping.mode' = 'name',
```

```
    'delta.minReaderVersion' = '2',
    'delta.minWriterVersion' = '5'
);
```

Schema evolution supports: - Adding new columns - Widening data types (e.g., INT to BIGINT) - Renaming columns (with column mapping enabled) - Dropping columns (with column mapping enabled)

> **Exam Tip:** Schema enforcement is **on by default.** Schema evolution must be explicitly enabled with `mergeSchema = true` or table properties. Know that `overwriteSchema = true` is used to completely replace the schema (different from `mergeSchema`).

1.42 Constraints and Generated Columns

1.42.1 CHECK Constraints

```
-- Add a CHECK constraint
ALTER TABLE analytics.sales.orders ADD CONSTRAINT valid_quantity CHECK (quantity > 0);
ALTER TABLE analytics.sales.orders ADD CONSTRAINT valid_price CHECK (unit_price >= 0);

-- Drop a constraint
ALTER TABLE analytics.sales.orders DROP CONSTRAINT valid_quantity;
```

1.42.2 NOT NULL Constraints

```
-- Define NOT NULL during creation
CREATE TABLE analytics.sales.orders (
    order_id BIGINT NOT NULL,
    customer_id BIGINT NOT NULL,
    amount DECIMAL(10,2)
);

-- Add NOT NULL to existing column
ALTER TABLE analytics.sales.orders ALTER COLUMN customer_id SET NOT NULL;
```

1.42.3 Generated Columns

Generated columns are computed automatically from other columns:

```
CREATE TABLE analytics.sales.orders (
    order_id BIGINT,
    quantity INT,
    unit_price DECIMAL(10,2),
    total_amount DECIMAL(10,2) GENERATED ALWAYS AS (quantity * unit_price),
    order_date DATE,
    order_year INT GENERATED ALWAYS AS (YEAR(order_date)),
    order_month INT GENERATED ALWAYS AS (MONTH(order_date))
);
```

Generated columns are useful for: - Deriving partition columns from existing columns - Computing frequently needed values once instead of at query time - Enforcing business rules at the storage level

---

1.43 Table Properties

Delta tables support a rich set of configurable properties:

```
-- Set table properties
ALTER TABLE analytics.sales.orders SET TBLPROPERTIES (
    'delta.autoOptimize.optimizeWrite' = 'true',
    'delta.autoOptimize.autoCompact' = 'true',
    'delta.logRetentionDuration' = 'interval 30 days',
    'delta.deletedFileRetentionDuration' = 'interval 7 days',
    'delta.dataSkippingNumIndexedCols' = '8'
);

-- View table properties
SHOW TBLPROPERTIES analytics.sales.orders;

-- Describe table details
DESCRIBE DETAIL analytics.sales.orders;
DESCRIBE EXTENDED analytics.sales.orders;
```

Key table properties:

Property	Default	Description
`delta.autoOptimize.optimizeWrite`	false	Coalesce small files on write
`delta.autoOptimize.autoCompact`	false	Automatically compact small files
`delta.logRetentionDuration`	30 days	How long to retain transaction log entries
`delta.deletedFileRetentionDuration`	7 days	VACUUM retention period
`delta.dataSkippingNumIndexedCols`	32	Number of columns to index for data skipping

Exam Tip: `optimizeWrite` and `autoCompact` together help prevent the small files problem. `optimizeWrite` coalesces files during writes; `autoCompact` triggers small compaction runs after writes. Know the difference between these and manual `OPTIMIZE`.

1.44 Chapter Summary

In this chapter, you learned:

- Delta Lake adds **ACID transactions, time travel, and DML support** to data lakes via a transaction log
- The **transaction log** records all changes as JSON commits with checkpoints every 10 versions
- **MERGE** enables upsert patterns with matched/not-matched clauses
- **Time travel** allows querying historical versions by version number or timestamp
- **OPTIMIZE** compacts small files; **Z-ORDER** co-locates related data; **VACUUM** removes old files
- **Schema enforcement** prevents bad data; **schema evolution** allows controlled schema changes
- **Constraints** (CHECK, NOT NULL) and **generated columns** enforce data quality at the storage level

---

1.45 Practice Questions

Question 1: How often does Delta Lake create checkpoint files in the transaction log by default?

A. Every commit B. Every 5 commits C. Every 10 commits D. Every 100 commits

Question 2: A data engineer runs `VACUUM analytics.sales.orders RETAIN 48 HOURS`. What is the effect?

A. Time travel works for all versions B. Data files older than 48 hours are permanently deleted C. The operation fails because minimum retention is 168 hours D. Only transaction log entries are removed

Question 3: Which MERGE clause should be used to insert new records that do not have a match in the target table?

A. `WHEN MATCHED THEN INSERT` B. `WHEN NOT MATCHED THEN UPDATE` C. `WHEN NOT MATCHED THEN INSERT` D. `WHEN MATCHED THEN MERGE`

Question 4: A table has columns `order_date` (DATE) and `customer_id` (BIGINT). Queries frequently filter on both columns. What optimization should the data engineer apply?

A. `VACUUM analytics.sales.orders` B. `OPTIMIZE analytics.sales.orders ZORDER BY (order_date, customer_id)` C. `ALTER TABLE analytics.sales.orders SET TBLPROPERTIES ('delta.autoOptimize.optimizeWrite' = 'true')` D. `DESCRIBE HISTORY analytics.sales.orders`

Question 5: What happens when you try to append data with an extra column to a Delta table without enabling schema evolution?

A. The extra column is silently ignored B. The write succeeds and the new column is added C. The write fails with a schema mismatch error D. The extra column is added but filled with NULL for existing rows

Question 6: Which time travel syntax retrieves data as it existed at a specific timestamp?

A. `SELECT * FROM table VERSION AS OF '2026-03-01'` B. `SELECT * FROM table TIMESTAMP AS OF '2026-03-01'` C. `SELECT * FROM table AT TIMESTAMP '2026-03-01'` D. `SELECT * FROM table HISTORY '2026-03-01'`

Question 7: What is the primary benefit of the `optimizeWrite` table property?

A. It compacts existing small files in the table B. It coalesces partitions during write operations to reduce small files C. It enables Z-ORDER on write operations D. It automatically runs VACUUM after each write

Question 8: A data engineer creates a table with `CLUSTER BY (order_date, region)`. What optimization technique is being used?

A. Z-ORDER B. Partitioning C. Liquid Clustering D. Data skipping

Question 9: Which Delta Lake feature allows renaming and dropping columns?

A. Schema enforcement B. Schema evolution with `mergeSchema` C. Column mapping mode D. Generated columns

Question 10: What does the `RESTORE TABLE` command do?

A. Recovers a dropped table from the recycle bin B. Reverts a table to a previous version, creating a new commit C. Undoes the last VACUUM operation D. Resets table properties to defaults

---

1.46 Answer Explanations

Question 1: C. Delta Lake creates checkpoint files every 10 commits by default. Checkpoints consolidate the transaction log state into a single Parquet file, reducing the number of JSON files readers must process. Reference: Delta Lake transaction log documentation.

Question 2: B. VACUUM with `RETAIN 48 HOURS` deletes data files no longer referenced by the transaction log that are older than 48 hours. However, this requires setting `delta.retentionDurationCheck.enabled = false` because the default minimum is 168 hours (7 days). The operation will fail unless that check is disabled. Reference: Delta Lake VACUUM documentation.

Question 3: C. `WHEN NOT MATCHED THEN INSERT` handles records in the source that do not have matching records in the target. This is the "insert" part of an upsert operation. Reference: Delta Lake MERGE documentation.

Question 4: B. OPTIMIZE with ZORDER BY co-locates related data for the specified columns, enabling data skipping when those columns are used in WHERE clauses. This is the correct optimization for frequently filtered columns. Reference: Delta Lake OPTIMIZE and Z-ORDER documentation.

Question 5: C. Delta Lake enforces schema on write by default. If incoming data has an extra column not in the table schema, the write fails with a schema mismatch error. To allow the new column, use `mergeSchema = true`. Reference: Delta Lake schema enforcement documentation.

Question 6: B. The correct syntax is `TIMESTAMP AS OF`. `VERSION AS OF` uses an integer version number, not a timestamp. Reference: Delta Lake time travel documentation.

Question 7: B. The `optimizeWrite` property coalesces small partitions during write operations, producing fewer, larger files. It does not compact existing files (that is what `OPTIMIZE` or `autoCompact` does). Reference: Delta Lake auto-optimize documentation.

Question 8: C. The `CLUSTER BY` clause in a CREATE TABLE statement enables Liquid Clustering, which is a newer optimization that replaces both Z-ORDER and traditional partitioning. Reference: Databricks Liquid Clustering documentation.

Question 9: C. Column mapping mode (`delta.columnMapping.mode = 'name'`) enables renaming and dropping columns by mapping logical column names to physical column IDs in the data files. Reference: Delta Lake column mapping documentation.

Question 10: B. RESTORE TABLE reverts a table to a previous version by creating a new commit in the transaction log that points to the data files from the specified version. The old versions remain in the history. Reference: Delta Lake RESTORE documentation. # Chapter 5: Lakehouse Implementation Patterns

Meridian Certification Press—Microsoft DP-750: Implementing Azure Databricks Study Guide 2026

1.47 Learning Objectives

After completing this chapter, you will be able to:

- Design and implement the medallion architecture (bronze, silver, gold)
- Choose between managed and external tables for different use cases
- Implement partitioning strategies for large-scale tables
- Apply slowly changing dimension (SCD) patterns using Delta Lake
- Design multi-hop data pipelines with clear data quality boundaries
- Implement data lake organization best practices

1.48 The Medallion Architecture

The **medallion architecture** is the foundational design pattern for the Databricks Lakehouse. It organizes data into three progressive layers of quality and refinement:

1.48.1 Bronze Layer (Raw)

The bronze layer stores **raw, unprocessed data** exactly as it arrived from source systems:

- Data is ingested in its original format with minimal or no transformation
- Source metadata is appended (ingestion timestamp, source system, file name)
- Schema enforcement is relaxed to avoid data loss
- Supports replay and reprocessing from the raw source
- Acts as the single source of truth for all downstream layers

```
# Bronze layer ingestion example
from pyspark.sql.functions import current_timestamp, input_file_name, lit

raw_df = (spark.readStream
    .format("cloudFiles")
    .option("cloudFiles.format", "json")
    .option("cloudFiles.schemaLocation", "/checkpoints/orders_bronze/_schema")
    .load("/Volumes/raw/orders/incoming/"))

bronze_df = (raw_df
    .withColumn("_ingestion_timestamp", current_timestamp())
    .withColumn("_source_file", input_file_name())
    .withColumn("_source_system", lit("erp_orders")))

(bronze_df.writeStream
    .format("delta")
    .option("checkpointLocation", "/checkpoints/orders_bronze")
```

```
    .outputMode("append")
    .trigger(availableNow=True)
    .toTable("analytics.bronze.orders_raw"))

-- Bronze table with ingestion metadata
CREATE TABLE analytics.bronze.orders_raw (
    raw_payload STRING,
    _ingestion_timestamp TIMESTAMP,
    _source_file STRING,
    _source_system STRING
)
USING DELTA
TBLPROPERTIES (
    'delta.autoOptimize.optimizeWrite' = 'true',
    'quality' = 'bronze'
);
```

1.48.2 Silver Layer (Cleansed)

The silver layer contains **cleansed, validated, and conformed data**:

- Data types are enforced and standardized
- Duplicates are removed
- Null values are handled (filtered, filled, or flagged)
- Business keys are validated
- Data from multiple sources may be joined and conformed
- Represents the "enterprise view" of the data

```
# Silver layer transformation example
from pyspark.sql.functions import col, to_date, when, trim, upper

bronze_df = spark.table("analytics.bronze.orders_raw")

silver_df = (bronze_df
    # Parse and validate data types
    .withColumn("order_id", col("raw_payload.order_id").cast("bigint"))
    .withColumn("customer_id", col("raw_payload.customer_id").cast("bigint"))
    .withColumn("product_name", trim(col("raw_payload.product_name")))
    .withColumn("quantity", col("raw_payload.quantity").cast("int"))
    .withColumn("unit_price", col("raw_payload.unit_price").cast("decimal(10,2)"))
    .withColumn("order_date", to_date(col("raw_payload.order_date")))
    .withColumn("status", upper(trim(col("raw_payload.status"))))
    # Remove nulls on required fields
    .filter(col("order_id").isNotNull())
    .filter(col("customer_id").isNotNull())
    # Handle data quality
    .withColumn("quantity", when(col("quantity") < 0, 0).otherwise(col("quantity")))
    # Remove duplicates
    .dropDuplicates(["order_id"])
    # Select final columns
    .select("order_id", "customer_id", "product_name", "quantity",
            "unit_price", "order_date", "status", "_ingestion_timestamp")
)

# Write to silver using MERGE for idempotency
from delta.tables import DeltaTable

if spark.catalog.tableExists("analytics.silver.orders"):
    target = DeltaTable.forName(spark, "analytics.silver.orders")
    target.alias("t").merge(
```

```
        silver_df.alias("s"), "t.order_id = s.order_id"
    ).whenMatchedUpdateAll().whenNotMatchedInsertAll().execute()
else:
    silver_df.write.format("delta").saveAsTable("analytics.silver.orders")
```

1.48.3 Gold Layer (Business-Level Aggregates)

The gold layer contains **business-level aggregates and curated datasets** optimized for consumption:

- Purpose-built for specific business use cases, dashboards, or ML models
- Highly aggregated and denormalized for query performance
- May combine data from multiple silver tables
- Optimized with Z-ORDER or Liquid Clustering on common query patterns
- Often surfaced through SQL warehouses to BI tools

```
-- Gold layer: daily revenue summary
CREATE OR REPLACE TABLE analytics.gold.daily_revenue AS
SELECT
    o.order_date,
    c.customer_segment,
    p.product_category,
    COUNT(DISTINCT o.order_id) AS order_count,
    COUNT(DISTINCT o.customer_id) AS unique_customers,
    SUM(o.quantity) AS total_units,
    SUM(o.quantity * o.unit_price) AS gross_revenue,
    AVG(o.quantity * o.unit_price) AS avg_order_value
FROM analytics.silver.orders o
JOIN analytics.silver.customers c ON o.customer_id = c.customer_id
JOIN analytics.silver.products p ON o.product_name = p.product_name
WHERE o.status = 'COMPLETED'
GROUP BY o.order_date, c.customer_segment, p.product_category;

-- Optimize for common query patterns
OPTIMIZE analytics.gold.daily_revenue ZORDER BY (order_date, product_category);
```

Exam Tip: The medallion architecture is one of the most heavily tested topics on the DP-750. Know the purpose and characteristics of each layer: bronze (raw, append-only), silver (cleansed, conformed), gold (aggregated, business-ready). Questions often ask which layer a specific transformation belongs in.

1.48.4 Layer Comparison Summary

Aspect	Bronze	Silver	Gold
Data quality	Raw, as-is	Validated, cleansed	Curated, business-ready
Schema	Flexible	Enforced	Optimized, denormalized
Consumers	Data engineers	Data engineers, analysts	Business users, BI tools
Write pattern	Append-only	MERGE / upsert	Overwrite or MERGE
Update frequency	Real-time or micro-batch	Near real-time	Scheduled (hourly/daily)
Storage format	Delta (raw columns)	Delta (typed columns)	Delta (aggregated)

1.49 Catalog and Schema Organization

1.49.1 Environment-Based Organization

A common pattern uses separate catalogs for each environment:

```
-- Development environment
CREATE CATALOG dev;
CREATE SCHEMA dev.bronze;
CREATE SCHEMA dev.silver;
CREATE SCHEMA dev.gold;

-- Staging environment
CREATE CATALOG staging;
CREATE SCHEMA staging.bronze;
CREATE SCHEMA staging.silver;
CREATE SCHEMA staging.gold;

-- Production environment
CREATE CATALOG prod;
CREATE SCHEMA prod.bronze;
CREATE SCHEMA prod.silver;
CREATE SCHEMA prod.gold;
```

1.49.2 Domain-Based Organization

For larger organizations, domain-based catalogs may be more appropriate:

```
-- Sales domain
CREATE CATALOG sales;
CREATE SCHEMA sales.bronze;
CREATE SCHEMA sales.silver;
CREATE SCHEMA sales.gold;

-- Marketing domain
CREATE CATALOG marketing;
CREATE SCHEMA marketing.bronze;
CREATE SCHEMA marketing.silver;
CREATE SCHEMA marketing.gold;
```

1.49.3 Hybrid Organization

Many enterprises use a combination:

```
-- Production catalogs by domain
CREATE CATALOG prod_sales;
CREATE CATALOG prod_marketing;

-- Shared development catalog
CREATE CATALOG dev;
CREATE SCHEMA dev.sales_bronze;
CREATE SCHEMA dev.marketing_bronze;
```

Exam Tip: There is no single "correct" catalog organization pattern. The exam tests your ability to evaluate tradeoffs. Environment-based catalogs simplify promotion workflows; domain-based catalogs align with data ownership. Choose based on the scenario presented.

1.50 Partitioning Strategies

1.50.1 Traditional Partitioning

Delta Lake supports Hive-style partitioning for large tables:

```
-- Partition by date for time-series data
CREATE TABLE analytics.silver.events (
    event_id BIGINT,
    event_type STRING,
    user_id BIGINT,
    event_data STRING,
    event_date DATE
)
USING DELTA
PARTITIONED BY (event_date);
```

When to partition: - Tables larger than 1 TB - Queries almost always filter on the partition column - Partition column has low-to-medium cardinality (hundreds, not millions) - Each partition contains at least 1 GB of data

When NOT to partition: - Tables smaller than 1 TB - High-cardinality partition columns (millions of unique values) - Partitions would be very small (< 1 GB each) - Query patterns vary and do not consistently filter on one column

1.50.2 Liquid Clustering (Recommended)

For new tables, Liquid Clustering is generally preferred over traditional partitioning:

```
-- Liquid clustering replaces both partitioning and Z-ORDER
CREATE TABLE analytics.silver.events (
    event_id BIGINT,
    event_type STRING,
    user_id BIGINT,
    event_data STRING,
    event_date DATE
)
CLUSTER BY (event_date, event_type);
```

Liquid Clustering advantages over partitioning: - No need to choose partition columns upfront - Can be changed without rewriting the table - Works well with any cardinality - Incrementally optimized with OPTIMIZE - Eliminates the small file problem associated with over-partitioning

> **Exam Tip:** For the DP-750 exam, know that **Liquid Clustering is the recommended approach for new tables.** Traditional partitioning is still valid and may appear in legacy scenarios or when asked about tables larger than 1 TB with a clear single-column filter pattern.

1.51 Slowly Changing Dimensions (SCD)

1.51.1 SCD Type 1 (Overwrite)

SCD Type 1 overwrites old values with new values, maintaining no history:

```
-- SCD Type 1: Overwrite with MERGE
MERGE INTO analytics.silver.customers AS target
USING staging.customer_updates AS source
ON target.customer_id = source.customer_id
WHEN MATCHED THEN
    UPDATE SET
```

```
        target.name = source.name,
        target.email = source.email,
        target.phone = source.phone,
        target.updated_at = current_timestamp()
WHEN NOT MATCHED THEN
    INSERT (customer_id, name, email, phone, created_at, updated_at)
    VALUES (source.customer_id, source.name, source.email, source.phone,
            current_timestamp(), current_timestamp());
```

1.51.2 SCD Type 2 (Historical Tracking)

SCD Type 2 preserves historical records by creating new rows for changes:

```
-- SCD Type 2 implementation
-- Step 1: Close existing records that have changes
MERGE INTO analytics.silver.customers_scd2 AS target
USING (
    SELECT s.*, t.customer_id AS existing_id
    FROM staging.customer_updates s
    LEFT JOIN analytics.silver.customers_scd2 t
        ON s.customer_id = t.customer_id AND t.is_current = TRUE
    WHERE t.customer_id IS NOT NULL
      AND (s.name != t.name OR s.email != t.email OR s.phone != t.phone)
) AS changes
ON target.customer_id = changes.existing_id AND target.is_current = TRUE
WHEN MATCHED THEN
    UPDATE SET
        target.is_current = FALSE,
        target.end_date = current_timestamp();

-- Step 2: Insert new current records
INSERT INTO analytics.silver.customers_scd2
SELECT
    s.customer_id,
    s.name,
    s.email,
    s.phone,
    current_timestamp() AS start_date,
    NULL AS end_date,
    TRUE AS is_current
FROM staging.customer_updates s
WHERE NOT EXISTS (
    SELECT 1 FROM analytics.silver.customers_scd2 t
    WHERE t.customer_id = s.customer_id
      AND t.is_current = TRUE
      AND t.name = s.name AND t.email = s.email AND t.phone = s.phone
);
```

```
# SCD Type 2 with PySpark DeltaTable API
from delta.tables import DeltaTable
from pyspark.sql.functions import current_timestamp, lit, col

target = DeltaTable.forName(spark, "analytics.silver.customers_scd2")
updates = spark.table("staging.customer_updates")

# Close old records
target.alias("t").merge(
    updates.alias("s"),
    "t.customer_id = s.customer_id AND t.is_current = TRUE"
```

```
).whenMatchedUpdate(
    condition="s.name != t.name OR s.email != t.email",
    set={
        "is_current": lit(False),
        "end_date": current_timestamp()
    }
).execute()

# Insert new current records
new_records = (updates.alias("s")
    .join(
        spark.table("analytics.silver.customers_scd2")
            .filter(col("is_current") == True).alias("t"),
        (col("s.customer_id") == col("t.customer_id")) &
        (col("s.name") == col("t.name")) &
        (col("s.email") == col("t.email")),
        "left_anti"
    )
    .withColumn("start_date", current_timestamp())
    .withColumn("end_date", lit(None).cast("timestamp"))
    .withColumn("is_current", lit(True)))

new_records.write.format("delta").mode("append") \
    .saveAsTable("analytics.silver.customers_scd2")
```

Exam Tip: SCD Type 2 is a common exam topic, often combined with MERGE. Know that SCD Type 2 requires: (1) closing the old record by setting `is_current = FALSE` and `end_date`, then (2) inserting a new record with `is_current = TRUE`. The two-step approach is important.

1.52 Data Quality Patterns

1.52.1 Quarantine Pattern

Route bad records to a quarantine table instead of dropping them:

```
from pyspark.sql.functions import col

raw_df = spark.table("analytics.bronze.orders_raw")

# Separate good and bad records
good_records = raw_df.filter(
    col("order_id").isNotNull() &
    col("customer_id").isNotNull() &
    (col("quantity") > 0) &
    (col("unit_price") >= 0)
)

bad_records = raw_df.filter(
    col("order_id").isNull() |
    col("customer_id").isNull() |
    (col("quantity") <= 0) |
    (col("unit_price") < 0)
)

# Write good records to silver
good_records.write.format("delta").mode("append") \
    .saveAsTable("analytics.silver.orders")
```

```
# Write bad records to quarantine for investigation
bad_records.write.format("delta").mode("append") \
    .saveAsTable("analytics.quarantine.orders_rejected")
```

1.52.2 Expectation-Based Quality

Delta Live Tables (covered in Chapter 10) provides built-in data quality expectations:

```
import dlt
from pyspark.sql.functions import col

@dlt.expect_or_drop("valid_order_id", "order_id IS NOT NULL")
@dlt.expect_or_fail("valid_quantity", "quantity > 0")
@dlt.expect("valid_price", "unit_price >= 0")
@dlt.table
def silver_orders():
    return spark.table("LIVE.bronze_orders")
```

1.53 Views and Materialized Views

1.53.1 Standard Views

Views provide a logical abstraction over tables without storing data:

```
-- Create a view for common queries
CREATE VIEW analytics.gold.active_customers AS
SELECT
    c.customer_id,
    c.name,
    c.email,
    COUNT(o.order_id) AS order_count,
    SUM(o.quantity * o.unit_price) AS total_spend
FROM analytics.silver.customers c
JOIN analytics.silver.orders o ON c.customer_id = o.customer_id
WHERE o.order_date >= date_sub(current_date(), 365)
GROUP BY c.customer_id, c.name, c.email;
```

1.53.2 Dynamic Views for Security

Dynamic views apply row-level or column-level security:

```
-- Row-level security with dynamic view
CREATE VIEW analytics.gold.my_orders AS
SELECT *
FROM analytics.silver.orders
WHERE owner = current_user();

-- Column-level masking with dynamic view
CREATE VIEW analytics.gold.customers_masked AS
SELECT
    customer_id,
    name,
    CASE
        WHEN is_member('pii-viewers') THEN email
```

```
        ELSE regexp_replace(email, '(.).*(@.*)', '$1***$2')
    END AS email,
    CASE
        WHEN is_member('pii-viewers') THEN phone
        ELSE 'XXX-XXX-' || right(phone, 4)
    END AS phone
FROM analytics.silver.customers;
```

Exam Tip: Dynamic views using `current_user()` and `is_member()` are a key mechanism for implementing row-level and column-level security in Unity Catalog. These functions are evaluated at query time, so different users see different results from the same view.

1.54 Chapter Summary

In this chapter, you learned:

- The **medallion architecture** organizes data into bronze (raw), silver (cleansed), and gold (aggregated) layers
- **Catalog/schema organization** can follow environment-based, domain-based, or hybrid patterns
- **Liquid Clustering** is recommended over traditional partitioning for new tables
- **SCD Type 1** overwrites with MERGE; **SCD Type 2** preserves history with current/end-date tracking
- **Quarantine patterns** separate bad records instead of dropping them
- **Dynamic views** enable row-level and column-level security through `current_user()` and `is_member()`

1.55 Practice Questions

Question 1: In the medallion architecture, which layer should contain raw, unprocessed data with ingestion metadata?

A. Gold B. Silver C. Bronze D. Platinum

Question 2: A data engineer needs to track historical changes to customer addresses over time. Which pattern should they implement?

A. SCD Type 1 B. SCD Type 2 C. Append-only logging D. Snapshot tables

Question 3: Which of the following is a characteristic of the silver layer?

A. Data is stored exactly as received from source systems B. Data is aggregated for specific business use cases C. Data is cleansed, validated, and conformed D. Data is optimized for machine learning training

Question 4: A table contains 500 GB of data. Queries filter on a `region` column that has 5 distinct values. Is traditional partitioning appropriate?

A. Yes, because each partition would contain approximately 100 GB B. No, because the table is too small for partitioning C. No, because 5 partitions is too few D. Yes, but only if combined with Z-ORDER

Question 5: What function is used in dynamic views to determine the currently logged-in user?

A. `session_user()` B. `current_user()` C. `get_user()` D. `identity()`

Question 6: A data engineer wants to organize Unity Catalog objects so that development and production data are fully separated. Which approach is recommended?

A. Use separate schemas within a single catalog B. Use separate catalogs for each environment C. Use separate metastores for each environment D. Use table-level tags to distinguish environments

Question 7: In SCD Type 2 using MERGE, what must happen to the existing current record when a change is detected?

A. It is deleted B. It is updated with new values (overwritten) C. Its `is_current` flag is set to FALSE and an `end_date` is set D. It is moved to an archive table

Question 8: Which of the following is NOT a recommended use case for the gold layer?

A. Pre-aggregated metrics for dashboards B. Denormalized tables for BI tools C. Raw data preservation for audit compliance D. Feature tables for machine learning models

---

1.56 Answer Explanations

Question 1: C. The bronze layer stores raw, unprocessed data with ingestion metadata such as timestamps and source file names. It acts as the foundation of the medallion architecture. Reference: Databricks medallion architecture documentation.

Question 2: B. SCD Type 2 preserves historical records by creating new rows when changes occur, with `is_current`, `start_date`, and `end_date` columns to track validity. SCD Type 1 would overwrite the old address without retaining history. Reference: Delta Lake SCD patterns.

Question 3: C. The silver layer contains cleansed, validated, and conformed data. It enforces data types, removes duplicates, and handles null values. Bronze is raw; gold is aggregated. Reference: Databricks medallion architecture.

Question 4: A. With 500 GB total and 5 partitions, each partition would contain approximately 100 GB, which exceeds the recommended minimum of 1 GB per partition. The low cardinality and large partition sizes make traditional partitioning appropriate. Reference: Delta Lake partitioning best practices.

Question 5: B. The `current_user()` function returns the identity of the user executing the query. It is used in dynamic views for row-level security. Reference: Databricks SQL functions documentation.

Question 6: B. Separate catalogs for each environment (dev, staging, prod) provide full isolation including separate permissions, making it the recommended approach for environment separation. Reference: Unity Catalog best practices.

Question 7: C. In SCD Type 2, when a change is detected, the existing current record must be "closed" by setting `is_current = FALSE` and populating the `end_date`. A new record is then inserted with `is_current = TRUE`. Reference: SCD Type 2 implementation patterns.

Question 8: C. Raw data preservation for audit compliance belongs in the bronze layer, not the gold layer. The gold layer is for business-ready aggregates, denormalized views, and curated datasets. Reference: Databricks medallion architecture documentation. # Chapter 6: Data Ingestion with Auto Loader and COPY INTO

Meridian Certification Press—Microsoft DP-750: Implementing Azure Databricks Study Guide 2026

1.57 Learning Objectives

After completing this chapter, you will be able to:

- Explain the difference between Auto Loader and COPY INTO
- Configure Auto Loader for streaming file ingestion
- Use COPY INTO for batch file ingestion
- Handle schema inference and evolution during ingestion
- Implement file notification mode for large-scale ingestion
- Troubleshoot common ingestion issues

1.58 Ingestion Overview

Data ingestion is the process of loading raw data from external sources into the lakehouse. Azure Databricks provides two primary mechanisms for file-based ingestion:

1. **Auto Loader (cloudFiles)**—A streaming-based approach that incrementally processes new files as they arrive
2. **COPY INTO**—A SQL-based batch command that loads files into an existing Delta table

Both tools are designed to load files from cloud storage (ADLS Gen2, Azure Blob Storage) into Delta tables, but they differ significantly in architecture, performance characteristics, and use cases.

1.58.1 When to Use Each Approach

Criteria	Auto Loader	COPY INTO
File volume	Millions of files	Thousands of files
Arrival pattern	Continuous / streaming	Batch / scheduled
Schema management	Automatic inference and evolution	Manual schema definition
State management	Built-in checkpoint	Built-in file tracking
Scalability	Highly scalable (file notification mode)	Limited by directory listing
Programming model	Structured Streaming (PySpark)	SQL command
Complexity	Moderate	Simple

Exam Tip: The exam frequently asks when to choose Auto Loader versus COPY INTO. The key differentiator is scale: Auto Loader is preferred for **millions of files** or **continuous ingestion**, while COPY INTO is simpler and suitable for **smaller, batch-oriented** scenarios.

1.59 Auto Loader (cloudFiles)

Auto Loader is the recommended ingestion mechanism for most production workloads. It uses Structured Streaming with a special `cloudFiles` data source to incrementally and efficiently process new files from cloud storage.

1.59.1 Basic Auto Loader Configuration

```
# Basic Auto Loader ingestion
df = (spark.readStream
    .format("cloudFiles")
    .option("cloudFiles.format", "json")
    .option("cloudFiles.schemaLocation", "/checkpoints/orders/_schema")
    .load("/Volumes/raw/orders/incoming/"))

(df.writeStream
    .format("delta")
    .option("checkpointLocation", "/checkpoints/orders/")
    .outputMode("append")
    .trigger(availableNow=True)
    .toTable("analytics.bronze.orders"))
```

Key parameters:

- `cloudFiles.format`—The format of source files (json, csv, parquet, avro, text, binaryFile)
- `cloudFiles.schemaLocation`—Where to store the inferred schema (required for schema inference)
- `checkpointLocation`—Where to store the streaming checkpoint (tracks processed files)

1.59.2 Supported File Formats

Auto Loader supports the following source formats:

Format	Option Value	Notes
JSON	`json`	Single-line or multi-line
CSV	`csv`	With header inference
Parquet	`parquet`	Columnar format
Avro	`avro`	Schema-embedded format
Text	`text`	One row per line
Binary	`binaryFile`	Images, PDFs, etc.
XML	`xml`	Requires additional parsing

Format	Option Value	Notes
ORC	`orc`	Hadoop columnar format

1.59.3 CSV-Specific Configuration

```
# Auto Loader with CSV files
df = (spark.readStream
    .format("cloudFiles")
    .option("cloudFiles.format", "csv")
    .option("header", "true")
    .option("inferSchema", "true")
    .option("cloudFiles.schemaLocation", "/checkpoints/csv_data/_schema")
    .option("sep", ",")
    .option("quote", '"')
    .option("escape", '"')
    .option("multiLine", "true")
    .load("/Volumes/raw/csv_data/"))
```

1.59.4 JSON-Specific Configuration

```
# Auto Loader with nested JSON
df = (spark.readStream
    .format("cloudFiles")
    .option("cloudFiles.format", "json")
    .option("cloudFiles.schemaLocation", "/checkpoints/json_data/_schema")
    .option("multiLine", "true")
    .option("cloudFiles.schemaEvolutionMode", "addNewColumns")
    .load("/Volumes/raw/json_data/"))
```

1.60 Auto Loader File Discovery Modes

Auto Loader supports two modes for discovering new files:

1.60.1 Directory Listing Mode (Default)

In directory listing mode, Auto Loader lists the files in the source directory to identify new files:

```
# Directory listing mode (default)
df = (spark.readStream
    .format("cloudFiles")
    .option("cloudFiles.format", "json")
    .option("cloudFiles.useNotifications", "false")  # default
    .option("cloudFiles.schemaLocation", "/checkpoints/schema/")
    .load("/Volumes/raw/data/"))
```

Characteristics: - Simple setup—no additional Azure infrastructure needed - Works well for directories with up to tens of thousands of files - Performance degrades with very large directories (millions of files) - Uses incremental listing with lexicographic ordering for efficiency

1.60.2 File Notification Mode

File notification mode uses Azure Event Grid and Queue Storage to receive notifications when new files arrive:

```
# File notification mode
df = (spark.readStream
    .format("cloudFiles")
    .option("cloudFiles.format", "json")
    .option("cloudFiles.useNotifications", "true")
    .option("cloudFiles.schemaLocation", "/checkpoints/schema/")
    # Azure-specific notification options
    .option("cloudFiles.resourceGroup", "rg-databricks")
    .option("cloudFiles.subscriptionId", "your-subscription-id")
    .option("cloudFiles.tenantId", "your-tenant-id")
    .option("cloudFiles.clientId", "your-client-id")
    .option("cloudFiles.clientSecret", dbutils.secrets.get("scope", "client-secret"))
    .load("abfss://container@storageaccount.dfs.core.windows.net/data/"))
```

Characteristics: - Highly scalable—handles millions of files efficiently - Near-real-time file discovery - Requires Azure Event Grid subscription and Queue Storage - Auto Loader can automatically set up the notification infrastructure - More complex setup but essential for large-scale production

> **Exam Tip:** Know the two file discovery modes. Directory listing is simpler but does not scale well. File notification mode scales to millions of files but requires Azure Event Grid. The exam may ask which mode to use for a given scenario—if the question mentions "millions of files" or "low latency," choose file notification mode.

1.61 Schema Inference and Evolution

1.61.1 Schema Inference

Auto Loader can infer the schema of incoming data automatically:

```
# Schema inference with schema location
df = (spark.readStream
    .format("cloudFiles")
    .option("cloudFiles.format", "json")
    .option("cloudFiles.inferColumnTypes", "true")
    .option("cloudFiles.schemaLocation", "/checkpoints/orders/_schema")
    .load("/Volumes/raw/orders/"))
```

The `schemaLocation` stores the inferred schema so that: - The schema is consistent across stream restarts - Schema changes are detected automatically - The schema does not need to be inferred from scratch each time

1.61.2 Schema Evolution

Auto Loader supports automatic schema evolution when new columns appear in source data:

```
# Enable schema evolution
df = (spark.readStream
    .format("cloudFiles")
    .option("cloudFiles.format", "json")
    .option("cloudFiles.schemaLocation", "/checkpoints/orders/_schema")
    .option("cloudFiles.schemaEvolutionMode", "addNewColumns")
    .load("/Volumes/raw/orders/"))
```

Schema evolution modes:

Mode	Behavior
`addNewColumns`	Automatically adds new columns to the schema; stream restarts to pick up changes
`rescue`	New/unexpected columns are placed in a `_rescued_data` column as JSON
`failOnNewColumns`	Stream fails when new columns are detected
`none`	No schema evolution; new columns are silently ignored

1.61.3 The Rescued Data Column

When schema evolution mode is set to `rescue` (or when columns do not match the expected schema), Auto Loader captures unexpected data in a special `_rescued_data` column:

```
# Enable rescued data column
df = (spark.readStream
    .format("cloudFiles")
    .option("cloudFiles.format", "json")
    .option("cloudFiles.schemaLocation", "/checkpoints/schema/")
    .option("cloudFiles.schemaEvolutionMode", "rescue")
    .load("/Volumes/raw/data/"))

# The _rescued_data column contains JSON strings of unexpected fields
# You can later parse and process rescued data
```

> **Exam Tip:** The `_rescued_data` column is a commonly tested concept. It captures data that does not match the inferred or provided schema, preventing data loss without failing the stream. Know that it stores unexpected columns as a JSON string.

1.61.4 Providing an Explicit Schema

For production pipelines, you may want to provide an explicit schema instead of relying on inference:

```
from pyspark.sql.types import *

order_schema = StructType([
    StructField("order_id", LongType(), False),
    StructField("customer_id", LongType(), True),
    StructField("product", StringType(), True),
    StructField("quantity", IntegerType(), True),
    StructField("price", DecimalType(10, 2), True),
    StructField("order_date", StringType(), True)
])

df = (spark.readStream
    .format("cloudFiles")
    .option("cloudFiles.format", "json")
    .schema(order_schema)
    .load("/Volumes/raw/orders/"))
```

When you provide an explicit schema: - `schemaLocation` is not required - Columns not in the schema go to `_rescued_data` (if enabled) - Schema evolution can still be enabled to add new columns

---

1.62 Auto Loader Trigger Modes

1.62.1 Continuous Processing

```
# Continuous streaming (always running)
(df.writeStream
    .format("delta")
    .option("checkpointLocation", "/checkpoints/orders/")
    .outputMode("append")
    .start())
```

1.62.2 Trigger Available Now

```
# Process all available files, then stop
(df.writeStream
    .format("delta")
    .option("checkpointLocation", "/checkpoints/orders/")
    .outputMode("append")
    .trigger(availableNow=True)
    .toTable("analytics.bronze.orders"))
```

`trigger(availableNow=True)` is the recommended trigger for batch-like processing with Auto Loader. It: - Processes all files that have arrived since the last run - Automatically stops when all available files are processed - Maintains checkpoint state for incremental processing - Is ideal for scheduled job runs

1.62.3 Trigger Once (Legacy)

```
# Legacy: Process one micro-batch, then stop
(df.writeStream
    .format("delta")
    .option("checkpointLocation", "/checkpoints/orders/")
    .outputMode("append")
    .trigger(once=True)
    .toTable("analytics.bronze.orders"))
```

> **Exam Tip:** `trigger(availableNow=True)` is preferred over `trigger(once=True)`. The `availableNow` trigger processes all available data in multiple micro-batches (more efficient for large volumes), while `once` processes everything in a single micro-batch. Know this distinction for the exam.

1.63 COPY INTO

1.63.1 Basic COPY INTO Syntax

`COPY INTO` is a SQL command that loads data from files into an existing Delta table:

```
-- Basic COPY INTO from JSON files
COPY INTO analytics.bronze.orders
FROM '/Volumes/raw/orders/incoming/'
FILEFORMAT = JSON
FORMAT_OPTIONS ('inferSchema' = 'true', 'multiLine' = 'true')
COPY_OPTIONS ('mergeSchema' = 'true');
```

1.63.2 COPY INTO with CSV Files

```
-- COPY INTO with CSV
COPY INTO analytics.bronze.sales_data
FROM '/Volumes/raw/sales/'
FILEFORMAT = CSV
FORMAT_OPTIONS (
    'header' = 'true',
    'inferSchema' = 'true',
    'delimiter' = ',',
    'quote' = '"',
    'escape' = '"'
)
COPY_OPTIONS ('mergeSchema' = 'true');
```

1.63.3 COPY INTO with Pattern Matching

```
-- Load only specific files using a pattern
COPY INTO analytics.bronze.orders
FROM '/Volumes/raw/orders/'
FILEFORMAT = JSON
PATTERN = '2026/03/*.json'
FORMAT_OPTIONS ('inferSchema' = 'true');
```

1.63.4 COPY INTO with Column Selection

```
-- Select and transform specific columns during ingestion
COPY INTO analytics.bronze.orders
FROM (
    SELECT
        _c0::BIGINT AS order_id,
        _c1::STRING AS product_name,
        _c2::DECIMAL(10,2) AS amount,
        _c3::DATE AS order_date,
        _metadata.file_path AS source_file,
        _metadata.file_modification_time AS file_mod_time
    FROM '/Volumes/raw/orders/'
)
FILEFORMAT = CSV
FORMAT_OPTIONS ('header' = 'false');
```

1.63.5 Key COPY INTO Behaviors

- **Idempotent:** COPY INTO tracks which files have already been loaded and will not reload them
- **Atomic:** Each COPY INTO execution is an atomic transaction
- **File tracking:** Uses the target table's transaction log to track loaded files
- **No checkpoint:** Unlike Auto Loader, COPY INTO does not use a separate checkpoint location

```
-- Force reload of already-loaded files
COPY INTO analytics.bronze.orders
FROM '/Volumes/raw/orders/'
FILEFORMAT = JSON
COPY_OPTIONS ('force' = 'true');
```

Exam Tip: COPY INTO is idempotent by default—running it multiple times will not create duplicate data because it tracks which files have been loaded. The `force = true` option overrides this behavior and reloads all files. This is a frequently tested behavior.

1.64 Ingestion Metadata

Both Auto Loader and COPY INTO can capture file-level metadata during ingestion:

1.64.1 Auto Loader Metadata

```
from pyspark.sql.functions import input_file_name, current_timestamp, col

df = (spark.readStream
    .format("cloudFiles")
    .option("cloudFiles.format", "json")
    .option("cloudFiles.schemaLocation", "/checkpoints/schema/")
    .load("/Volumes/raw/orders/"))

# Add ingestion metadata
enriched_df = (df
    .withColumn("_source_file", input_file_name())
    .withColumn("_ingestion_time", current_timestamp())
    .select("*", "_metadata.file_path", "_metadata.file_name",
            "_metadata.file_size", "_metadata.file_modification_time"))
```

1.64.2 COPY INTO Metadata

```
-- Access file metadata in COPY INTO
COPY INTO analytics.bronze.orders
FROM (
    SELECT
        *,
        _metadata.file_path AS source_path,
        _metadata.file_name AS source_filename,
        _metadata.file_size AS source_file_size,
        _metadata.file_modification_time AS source_mod_time
    FROM '/Volumes/raw/orders/'
)
FILEFORMAT = JSON;
```

The `_metadata` column is automatically available and includes: - `file_path`—Full path to the source file - `file_name`—Name of the source file - `file_size`—Size in bytes - `file_modification_time`—Last modification timestamp - `file_block_start` – Start offset for the block (multi-block files) - `file_block_length`—Length of the block

---

1.65 Error Handling and Troubleshooting

1.65.1 Handling Corrupt Records

```
# Auto Loader: capture corrupt records
df = (spark.readStream
    .format("cloudFiles")
    .option("cloudFiles.format", "json")
    .option("cloudFiles.schemaLocation", "/checkpoints/schema/")
    .option("mode", "PERMISSIVE")
    .option("columnNameOfCorruptRecord", "_corrupt_record")
    .load("/Volumes/raw/data/"))

# Filter corrupt records to quarantine
corrupt = df.filter(col("_corrupt_record").isNotNull())
valid = df.filter(col("_corrupt_record").isNull())
```

1.65.2 Parse Modes

Mode	Behavior
`PERMISSIVE` (default)	Sets corrupt fields to null; captures full record in `_corrupt_record`
`DROPMALFORMED`	Silently drops corrupt records
`FAILFAST`	Fails immediately on the first corrupt record

1.65.3 Common Issues and Solutions

Issue: "No files found" error - Verify the path exists and contains files - Check Unity Catalog permissions on the volume or external location - Confirm the file pattern matches actual file names

Issue: Schema mismatch - Check the inferred schema in the `schemaLocation` directory - Consider providing an explicit schema - Enable `_rescued_data` to capture mismatched columns

Issue: Duplicate data after restart - Verify the checkpoint location is consistent across runs - Do not change the checkpoint path between runs - Use `trigger(availableNow=True)` for consistent batch processing

---

1.66 Auto Loader vs. COPY INTO Decision Matrix

Factor	Auto Loader Wins	COPY INTO Wins
File count > 10,000	Yes	
Simple one-time load		Yes
Schema evolution needed	Yes	
SQL-only environment		Yes
Near real-time ingestion	Yes	
Ad-hoc data exploration		Yes
Production pipeline	Yes	
Minimal setup		Yes

Exam Tip: When in doubt on the exam, Auto Loader is usually the correct answer for production ingestion scenarios. COPY INTO is correct for simpler, batch-oriented, or SQL-only scenarios. Look for keywords like "incremental," "streaming," or "millions of files" (Auto Loader) versus "one-time load," "SQL command," or "simple batch" (COPY INTO).

1.67 Chapter Summary

In this chapter, you learned:

- **Auto Loader** uses Structured Streaming with the `cloudFiles` format for scalable, incremental file ingestion
- **COPY INTO** is a SQL command for batch file loading with built-in idempotency
- Auto Loader supports **directory listing** (simple) and **file notification** (scalable) modes
- **Schema inference** automatically detects data types; **schema evolution** handles new columns
- The **`_rescued_data`** column captures unexpected data without failing the stream
- **`trigger(availableNow=True)`** is preferred over `trigger(once=True)` for batch-like Auto Loader jobs
- Both tools support **ingestion metadata** through the `_metadata` column

---

1.68 Practice Questions

Question 1: A data engineer needs to ingest files from a directory that receives thousands of new files per hour. The pipeline must process files incrementally. Which approach should they use?

A. COPY INTO with a scheduled job B. Auto Loader with directory listing mode C. Auto Loader with file notification mode D. spark.read.format("json").load() in a loop

Question 2: What is the purpose of the `cloudFiles.schemaLocation` option in Auto Loader?

A. To specify where data files are stored B. To store the checkpoint for tracking processed files C. To store the inferred schema for consistency across stream restarts D. To define the output table location

Question 3: Which Auto Loader schema evolution mode places unexpected columns in a `_rescued_data` column?

A. `addNewColumns` B. `failOnNewColumns` C. `rescue` D. `none`

Question 4: A data engineer runs the same COPY INTO command twice. What happens on the second execution?

A. All data is loaded again, creating duplicates B. The command fails with an error C. Only new files since the first run are loaded D. The command succeeds but loads zero rows (files already tracked)

Question 5: Which trigger mode is recommended for Auto Loader when running as a scheduled batch job?

A. `trigger(once=True)` B. `trigger(availableNow=True)` C. `trigger(processingTime="1 minute")` D. No trigger (continuous)

Question 6: Auto Loader needs to process files from a storage account containing over 10 million files. Which file discovery mode should be used?

A. Directory listing mode B. File notification mode C. Manual file listing with dbutils.fs.ls() D. COPY INTO with PATTERN option

Question 7: Which `_metadata` field provides the full cloud storage path of the source file?

A. `_metadata.file_name` B. `_metadata.file_path` C. `_metadata.file_location` D. `_metadata.source_path`

Question 8: A COPY INTO command needs to reload files that were previously loaded. Which option should be used?

A. `COPY_OPTIONS ('reload' = 'true')` B. `COPY_OPTIONS ('force' = 'true')` C. `COPY_OPTIONS ('idempotent' = 'false')` D. `COPY_OPTIONS ('overwrite' = 'true')`

Question 9: What is the default parse mode for handling corrupt records in Auto Loader?

A. FAILFAST B. DROPMALFORMED C. PERMISSIVE D. IGNORE

Question 10: Which Auto Loader option should be set to `true` to enable automatic data type inference for columns?

A. `cloudFiles.inferSchema` B. `cloudFiles.inferColumnTypes` C. `cloudFiles.autoDetectTypes` D. `cloudFiles.schemaInference`

1.69 Answer Explanations

Question 1: C. With thousands of new files per hour, Auto Loader with file notification mode is the best choice. File notification mode uses Azure Event Grid for near-real-time, scalable file discovery without expensive directory listings. Reference: Auto Loader file notification mode documentation.

Question 2: C. The `schemaLocation` stores the inferred schema so it remains consistent across stream restarts. Without it, the schema would need to be re-inferred each time, potentially causing inconsistencies. The checkpoint location (separate option) tracks processed files. Reference: Auto Loader schema inference documentation.

Question 3: C. The `rescue` mode places unexpected or schema-mismatched columns into a `_rescued_data` column as a JSON string. This prevents data loss without failing the stream. Reference: Auto Loader schema evolution documentation.

Question 4: D. COPY INTO is idempotent by default. It tracks which files have been loaded and skips them on subsequent runs. The second execution succeeds but loads zero new rows. Reference: COPY INTO documentation.

Question 5: B. `trigger(availableNow=True)` is recommended for scheduled batch jobs. It processes all available files across multiple micro-batches and then stops, providing better efficiency than `trigger(once=True)` which processes everything in a single batch. Reference: Structured Streaming trigger documentation.

Question 6: B. File notification mode uses Azure Event Grid to receive notifications about new files, avoiding expensive directory listings. For 10+ million files, directory listing mode would be extremely slow. Reference: Auto Loader file discovery modes.

Question 7: B. The `_metadata.file_path` field contains the full cloud storage path of the source file. `file_name` contains only the filename without the directory path. Reference: Auto Loader metadata documentation.

Question 8: B. The `force = true` copy option forces COPY INTO to reload all files, even those that were previously loaded. This overrides the default idempotent behavior. Reference: COPY INTO options documentation.

Question 9: C. PERMISSIVE is the default parse mode. It sets corrupt fields to null and optionally captures the full corrupt record in a designated column. Reference: Spark data source read modes.

Question 10: B. The `cloudFiles.inferColumnTypes` option enables automatic type inference for columns. When set to true, Auto Loader infers appropriate data types instead of reading all columns as strings. Reference: Auto Loader configuration options. # Chapter 7: Data Transformation with Spark SQL and PySpark

Meridian Certification Press—Microsoft DP-750: Implementing Azure Databricks Study Guide 2026

1.70 Learning Objectives

After completing this chapter, you will be able to:

- Write transformations using both Spark SQL and the PySpark DataFrame API
- Apply common transformation operations: select, filter, aggregate, and sort
- Work with complex data types including arrays, maps, and structs
- Handle null values and type conversions
- Use built-in functions for strings, dates, and conditional logic
- Create and manage temporary views for SQL-based analysis

1.71 The Two APIs: Spark SQL and PySpark DataFrames

Azure Databricks supports two primary interfaces for data transformation, both of which execute on the same underlying Spark engine and produce identical query plans:

Spark SQL: Standard SQL syntax executed through `spark.sql()` or in SQL notebook cells.

PySpark DataFrame API: A Python-based fluent API for building transformations programmatically.

```
# PySpark DataFrame API
df = (spark.table("analytics.silver.orders")
    .filter(col("status") == "COMPLETED")
    .groupBy("product_name")
    .agg(sum("quantity").alias("total_qty"))
```

```
    .orderBy(col("total_qty").desc()))
```

```sql
-- Equivalent Spark SQL
SELECT product_name, SUM(quantity) AS total_qty
FROM analytics.silver.orders
WHERE status = 'COMPLETED'
GROUP BY product_name
ORDER BY total_qty DESC;
```

> **Exam Tip:** Both APIs produce the same execution plan and performance. The exam tests both SQL and PySpark syntax. Make sure you are comfortable reading and writing transformations in either form.

1.72 Reading Data

1.72.1 Reading from Tables

```python
# Read a Unity Catalog table
df = spark.table("analytics.silver.orders")

# Read with SQL
df = spark.sql("SELECT * FROM analytics.silver.orders")
```

1.72.2 Reading from Files

```python
# Read CSV
df_csv = (spark.read
    .option("header", "true")
    .option("inferSchema", "true")
    .csv("/Volumes/analytics/raw/data.csv"))

# Read JSON
df_json = spark.read.json("/Volumes/analytics/raw/data.json")

# Read Parquet
df_parquet = spark.read.parquet("/Volumes/analytics/raw/data.parquet")

# Read Delta
df_delta = spark.read.format("delta").load("/path/to/delta-table")
```

1.72.3 Creating Temporary Views

Temporary views make DataFrames accessible via SQL:

```python
# Create a temporary view
df.createOrReplaceTempView("orders_temp")

# Query using SQL
result = spark.sql("""
    SELECT product_name, COUNT(*) as order_count
    FROM orders_temp
    GROUP BY product_name
```

```
""")

# Global temporary views are accessible across notebooks in the same cluster
df.createOrReplaceGlobalTempView("orders_global")
# Access with: SELECT * FROM global_temp.orders_global
```

> **Exam Tip:** Temporary views are scoped to the SparkSession (notebook). Global temporary views are scoped to the cluster and accessed via the `global_temp` database. Know the difference and the syntax for each.

1.73 Core Transformations

1.73.1 SELECT and Column Operations

```python
from pyspark.sql.functions import col, lit, concat, upper, round

# Select specific columns
df.select("order_id", "customer_id", "amount")

# Select with expressions
df.select(
    col("order_id"),
    col("customer_id"),
    (col("quantity") * col("unit_price")).alias("total_amount"),
    upper(col("product_name")).alias("product_upper"),
    lit("USD").alias("currency")
)

# Add a new column
df.withColumn("total_amount", col("quantity") * col("unit_price"))

# Rename a column
df.withColumnRenamed("unit_price", "price_per_unit")

# Drop a column
df.drop("internal_code")
```

```sql
-- SQL equivalents
SELECT
    order_id,
    customer_id,
    quantity * unit_price AS total_amount,
    UPPER(product_name) AS product_upper,
    'USD' AS currency
FROM analytics.silver.orders;
```

1.73.2 Filtering (WHERE)

```python
from pyspark.sql.functions import col

# Simple filter
df.filter(col("status") == "COMPLETED")
df.filter(col("amount") > 100)
```

```python
# Multiple conditions
df.filter(
    (col("status") == "COMPLETED") &
    (col("amount") > 100) &
    (col("order_date") >= "2026-01-01")
)

# Using where (alias for filter)
df.where(col("status").isin("COMPLETED", "SHIPPED"))

# NOT condition
df.filter(~col("status").isin("CANCELLED", "RETURNED"))

# LIKE pattern matching
df.filter(col("product_name").like("%Widget%"))

# BETWEEN
df.filter(col("amount").between(50, 200))

# IS NULL / IS NOT NULL
df.filter(col("email").isNotNull())
```

```sql
-- SQL filtering
SELECT * FROM analytics.silver.orders
WHERE status = 'COMPLETED'
  AND amount > 100
  AND order_date >= '2026-01-01'
  AND product_name LIKE '%Widget%';
```

1.73.3 Sorting (ORDER BY)

```python
from pyspark.sql.functions import col, desc, asc

# Sort ascending (default)
df.orderBy("order_date")

# Sort descending
df.orderBy(col("amount").desc())

# Multiple sort columns
df.orderBy(col("order_date").desc(), col("amount").asc())

# Sort with nulls handling
df.orderBy(col("amount").desc_nulls_last())
```

1.73.4 Deduplication

```python
# Remove exact duplicate rows
df.distinct()

# Remove duplicates based on specific columns (keeps first occurrence)
df.dropDuplicates(["customer_id", "order_date"])
```

```sql
-- SQL deduplication
SELECT DISTINCT * FROM analytics.silver.orders;
```

```sql
-- Dedup on specific columns using ROW_NUMBER
SELECT * FROM (
    SELECT *,
        ROW_NUMBER() OVER (
            PARTITION BY customer_id, order_date
            ORDER BY _ingestion_timestamp DESC
        ) AS rn
    FROM analytics.silver.orders
)
WHERE rn = 1;
```

1.74 Aggregations

1.74.1 Basic Aggregations

```python
from pyspark.sql.functions import count, sum, avg, min, max, countDistinct

# Global aggregation
df.agg(
    count("*").alias("total_orders"),
    sum("amount").alias("total_revenue"),
    avg("amount").alias("avg_order_value"),
    min("order_date").alias("first_order"),
    max("order_date").alias("last_order"),
    countDistinct("customer_id").alias("unique_customers")
)

# Group by aggregation
df.groupBy("product_category").agg(
    count("order_id").alias("order_count"),
    sum("quantity").alias("total_units"),
    round(avg("unit_price"), 2).alias("avg_price")
)
```

```sql
-- SQL aggregation
SELECT
    product_category,
    COUNT(order_id) AS order_count,
    SUM(quantity) AS total_units,
    ROUND(AVG(unit_price), 2) AS avg_price
FROM analytics.silver.orders
GROUP BY product_category
HAVING COUNT(order_id) > 10
ORDER BY total_units DESC;
```

1.74.2 Multiple Grouping

```python
# Group by multiple columns
df.groupBy("product_category", "status").agg(
    count("*").alias("count"),
    sum("amount").alias("total")
)
```

```python
# Cube (all combinations of grouping columns)
df.cube("product_category", "region").agg(
    sum("amount").alias("total")
)

# Rollup (hierarchical grouping)
df.rollup("year", "quarter", "month").agg(
    sum("amount").alias("total")
)
```

```sql
-- ROLLUP for hierarchical totals
SELECT year, quarter, month, SUM(amount) AS total
FROM analytics.silver.orders
GROUP BY ROLLUP(year, quarter, month);

-- CUBE for all dimension combinations
SELECT product_category, region, SUM(amount) AS total
FROM analytics.silver.orders
GROUP BY CUBE(product_category, region);
```

Exam Tip: Know the difference between `GROUP BY`, `ROLLUP`, and `CUBE`. `GROUP BY` produces one row per group. `ROLLUP` adds hierarchical subtotals. `CUBE` produces all possible combinations of grouping columns. These are common exam topics.

1.75 Built-In Functions

1.75.1 String Functions

```python
from pyspark.sql.functions import (
    col, upper, lower, trim, ltrim, rtrim,
    length, substring, concat, concat_ws,
    regexp_replace, regexp_extract, split,
    lpad, rpad, initcap, reverse
)

df.select(
    upper(col("name")).alias("upper_name"),
    lower(col("email")).alias("lower_email"),
    trim(col("address")).alias("trimmed_address"),
    length(col("name")).alias("name_length"),
    substring(col("phone"), 1, 3).alias("area_code"),
    concat(col("first_name"), lit(" "), col("last_name")).alias("full_name"),
    concat_ws(", ", col("city"), col("state"), col("zip")).alias("full_address"),
    regexp_replace(col("phone"), "[^0-9]", "").alias("digits_only"),
    regexp_extract(col("email"), r"@(.+)", 1).alias("domain"),
    split(col("tags"), ",").alias("tag_array"),
    initcap(col("name")).alias("title_case")
)
```

```sql
-- SQL string functions
SELECT
    UPPER(name) AS upper_name,
    LOWER(email) AS lower_email,
    TRIM(address) AS trimmed_address,
```

```
    LENGTH(name) AS name_length,
    SUBSTRING(phone, 1, 3) AS area_code,
    CONCAT(first_name, ' ', last_name) AS full_name,
    CONCAT_WS(', ', city, state, zip) AS full_address,
    REGEXP_REPLACE(phone, '[^0-9]', '') AS digits_only,
    REGEXP_EXTRACT(email, '@(.+)', 1) AS domain,
    SPLIT(tags, ',') AS tag_array,
    INITCAP(name) AS title_case
FROM analytics.silver.customers;
```

1.75.2 Date and Timestamp Functions

```
from pyspark.sql.functions import (
    current_date, current_timestamp, date_format,
    year, month, dayofmonth, dayofweek, dayofyear,
    date_add, date_sub, datediff, months_between,
    to_date, to_timestamp, unix_timestamp, from_unixtime,
    date_trunc, last_day, next_day, trunc
)

df.select(
    current_date().alias("today"),
    current_timestamp().alias("now"),
    year(col("order_date")).alias("order_year"),
    month(col("order_date")).alias("order_month"),
    dayofweek(col("order_date")).alias("day_of_week"),
    date_format(col("order_date"), "yyyy-MM-dd").alias("formatted_date"),
    date_add(col("order_date"), 30).alias("due_date"),
    datediff(current_date(), col("order_date")).alias("days_since_order"),
    months_between(current_date(), col("order_date")).alias("months_since"),
    date_trunc("month", col("order_date")).alias("month_start"),
    to_date(col("date_string"), "MM/dd/yyyy").alias("parsed_date"),
    to_timestamp(col("ts_string"), "yyyy-MM-dd HH:mm:ss").alias("parsed_ts")
)
```

```
-- SQL date functions
SELECT
    CURRENT_DATE() AS today,
    YEAR(order_date) AS order_year,
    MONTH(order_date) AS order_month,
    DATE_FORMAT(order_date, 'yyyy-MM-dd') AS formatted_date,
    DATE_ADD(order_date, 30) AS due_date,
    DATEDIFF(CURRENT_DATE(), order_date) AS days_since_order,
    DATE_TRUNC('month', order_date) AS month_start,
    TO_DATE(date_string, 'MM/dd/yyyy') AS parsed_date
FROM analytics.silver.orders;
```

Exam Tip: Date functions are heavily tested. Know `to_date()` and `to_timestamp()` format strings (Java SimpleDateFormat patterns like `yyyy-MM-dd`). Also know `datediff()` returns an integer number of days, while `months_between()` returns a decimal number of months.

1.75.3 Conditional Functions

```
from pyspark.sql.functions import when, coalesce, isnull, col

# CASE WHEN equivalent
```

```
df.withColumn("tier",
    when(col("total_spend") > 10000, "platinum")
    .when(col("total_spend") > 5000, "gold")
    .when(col("total_spend") > 1000, "silver")
    .otherwise("bronze")
)

# COALESCE - returns first non-null value
df.withColumn("contact",
    coalesce(col("mobile_phone"), col("home_phone"), col("work_phone"))
)

# NULL handling
df.withColumn("has_email", col("email").isNotNull())
df.fillna({"quantity": 0, "status": "unknown"})
df.na.fill({"amount": 0.0})
df.na.drop(subset=["customer_id", "order_id"])
```

```
-- SQL CASE WHEN
SELECT *,
    CASE
        WHEN total_spend > 10000 THEN 'platinum'
        WHEN total_spend > 5000 THEN 'gold'
        WHEN total_spend > 1000 THEN 'silver'
        ELSE 'bronze'
    END AS tier,
    COALESCE(mobile_phone, home_phone, work_phone) AS contact,
    IFNULL(quantity, 0) AS quantity_clean,
    NULLIF(status, '') AS status_clean
FROM analytics.silver.customers;
```

1.76 Working with Complex Types

1.76.1 Structs

```
from pyspark.sql.functions import col, struct

# Access struct fields
df.select(
    col("address.street"),
    col("address.city"),
    col("address.state"),
    col("address.zip")
)

# Create a struct
df.withColumn("full_address",
    struct(
        col("street").alias("street"),
        col("city").alias("city"),
        col("state").alias("state"),
        col("zip").alias("zip")
    )
)
```

```
-- SQL struct access
SELECT
    address.street,
    address.city,
    address.state,
    address.zip,
    STRUCT(street, city, state, zip) AS full_address
FROM analytics.silver.customers;
```

1.76.2 Arrays

```
from pyspark.sql.functions import (
    array, explode, explode_outer, posexplode,
    array_contains, size, array_distinct, array_sort,
    flatten, array_union, array_intersect, array_except,
    collect_list, collect_set, element_at
)

# Explode array into rows
df.select("order_id", explode("items").alias("item"))

# explode_outer preserves rows where array is null/empty
df.select("order_id", explode_outer("items").alias("item"))

# Array operations
df.select(
    size(col("tags")).alias("num_tags"),
    array_contains(col("tags"), "urgent").alias("is_urgent"),
    array_distinct(col("tags")).alias("unique_tags"),
    element_at(col("tags"), 1).alias("first_tag")
)

# Aggregate into arrays
df.groupBy("customer_id").agg(
    collect_list("product_name").alias("products_ordered"),
    collect_set("product_category").alias("categories")
)
```

```
-- SQL array operations
SELECT
    order_id,
    EXPLODE(items) AS item
FROM analytics.silver.orders;

SELECT
    customer_id,
    SIZE(tags) AS num_tags,
    ARRAY_CONTAINS(tags, 'urgent') AS is_urgent,
    ELEMENT_AT(tags, 1) AS first_tag,
    COLLECT_LIST(product_name) AS all_products
FROM analytics.silver.orders
GROUP BY customer_id;
```

1.76.3 Maps

```
from pyspark.sql.functions import (
```

```
    create_map, map_keys, map_values, map_from_arrays,
    col, element_at
)

# Access map values
df.select(
    element_at(col("properties"), "color").alias("color"),
    map_keys(col("properties")).alias("property_keys"),
    map_values(col("properties")).alias("property_values")
)

# Create a map from columns
df.withColumn("dimensions",
    create_map(
        lit("width"), col("width"),
        lit("height"), col("height"),
        lit("depth"), col("depth")
    )
)
```

```
-- SQL map operations
SELECT
    properties['color'] AS color,
    MAP_KEYS(properties) AS all_keys,
    MAP_VALUES(properties) AS all_values
FROM analytics.silver.products;
```

Exam Tip: Complex types (arrays, maps, structs) are frequently tested. Know how to `EXPLODE` arrays into rows, access struct fields with dot notation, and access map values with bracket notation. Also know the difference between `explode()` (drops nulls) and `explode_outer()` (preserves nulls).

1.77 Type Conversions

```
from pyspark.sql.functions import col

# Cast column types
df.select(
    col("quantity").cast("integer"),
    col("price").cast("decimal(10,2)"),
    col("order_date").cast("date"),
    col("created_at").cast("timestamp"),
    col("is_active").cast("boolean"),
    col("order_id").cast("string")
)
```

```
-- SQL casting
SELECT
    CAST(quantity AS INT),
    CAST(price AS DECIMAL(10,2)),
    CAST(order_date AS DATE),
    CAST(created_at AS TIMESTAMP),
    CAST(is_active AS BOOLEAN),
    quantity::INT,          ---shorthand syntax
    price::DECIMAL(10,2)    ---shorthand syntax
FROM analytics.silver.orders;
```

1.78 Writing Transformed Data

```
# Write to a Delta table (append)
transformed_df.write.format("delta").mode("append") \
    .saveAsTable("analytics.silver.orders_cleaned")

# Write with overwrite
transformed_df.write.format("delta").mode("overwrite") \
    .saveAsTable("analytics.gold.daily_summary")

# Write with partition
transformed_df.write.format("delta").mode("overwrite") \
    .partitionBy("order_year", "order_month") \
    .saveAsTable("analytics.silver.orders_partitioned")

# Insert overwrite specific partitions
transformed_df.write.format("delta").mode("overwrite") \
    .option("replaceWhere", "order_date >= '2026-03-01'") \
    .saveAsTable("analytics.silver.orders")
```

```
-- SQL write operations
CREATE OR REPLACE TABLE analytics.gold.daily_summary AS
SELECT order_date, SUM(amount) AS total
FROM analytics.silver.orders
GROUP BY order_date;

-- Insert into existing table
INSERT INTO analytics.silver.orders_cleaned
SELECT * FROM staging.new_orders WHERE is_valid = TRUE;

-- Insert overwrite (replace matching partitions)
INSERT OVERWRITE analytics.silver.orders
SELECT * FROM staging.corrected_orders
WHERE order_date >= '2026-03-01';
```

> **Exam Tip:** Know the `replaceWhere` option for selectively overwriting partitions. It is more efficient than a full overwrite when you only need to update a subset of the data. The exam often presents scenarios where you need to re-process a specific date range without affecting other data.

1.79 Chapter Summary

In this chapter, you learned:

- Spark SQL and PySpark DataFrame API are **interchangeable** and produce identical execution plans
- **Temporary views** make DataFrames accessible via SQL; global temporary views span notebooks on the same cluster
- Core transformations include **select**, **filter**, **aggregate**, **sort**, and **deduplication**
- Built-in functions cover **strings** (upper, trim, regex), **dates** (datediff, date_trunc, to_date), and **conditionals** (when/otherwise, coalesce)
- Complex types include **structs** (dot notation), **arrays** (explode, array_contains), and **maps** (bracket notation)
- Data is written with modes: **append**, **overwrite**, **ignore**, **error**
- `replaceWhere` enables **selective partition overwriting**

1.80 Practice Questions

Question 1: What is the difference between `explode()` and `explode_outer()` when applied to an array column?

A. `explode()` creates one row per element; `explode_outer()` creates a single row with all elements B. `explode()` drops rows where the array is null; `explode_outer()` preserves them with null values C. `explode_outer()` works only with arrays of structs D. There is no functional difference; they are aliases

Question 2: Which function returns the first non-null value from a list of columns?

A. `IFNULL()` B. `NULLIF()` C. `COALESCE()` D. `NVL2()`

Question 3: A data engineer needs to convert the string "03/15/2026" to a DATE type. Which expression is correct?

A. `TO_DATE('03/15/2026', 'dd/MM/yyyy')` B. `TO_DATE('03/15/2026', 'MM/dd/yyyy')` C. `CAST('03/15/2026' AS DATE)` D. `DATE('03/15/2026')`

Question 4: What does `GROUP BY ROLLUP(year, quarter, month)` produce that `GROUP BY year, quarter, month` does not?

A. All possible combinations of the grouping columns B. Hierarchical subtotals and a grand total C. Only the grand total D. Results sorted by the grouping columns

Question 5: Which PySpark method creates a view that is accessible from other notebooks on the same cluster?

A. `createOrReplaceTempView()` B. `createOrReplaceGlobalTempView()` C. `createOrReplaceView()` D. `createClusterView()`

Question 6: A DataFrame has a column `properties` of type MAP<STRING, STRING>. Which expression retrieves the value for key "color"?

A. `col("properties").getItem("color")` B. `col("properties.color")` C. `map_get(col("properties"), "color")` D. Both A and the SQL equivalent `properties['color']` are correct

Question 7: Which write option allows overwriting only rows matching a specific condition in a Delta table?

A. `partitionOverwriteMode` B. `replaceWhere` C. `overwriteFilter` D. `conditionalOverwrite`

Question 8: What is the return type of the `datediff()` function?

A. DECIMAL B. INTERVAL C. INTEGER D. STRING

1.81 Answer Explanations

Question 1: B. `explode()` drops rows where the array column is null or empty. `explode_outer()` preserves those rows, outputting null for the exploded column. This is important when you need to retain records even if they have no array elements. Reference: PySpark explode documentation.

Question 2: C. `COALESCE()` returns the first non-null value from its arguments. `IFNULL()` handles only two arguments. `NULLIF()` returns null if two values are equal. Reference: Spark SQL functions documentation.

Question 3: B. The format string must match the input: month (03) = MM, day (15) = dd, year (2026) = yyyy. So the correct format is `MM/dd/yyyy`. The CAST option would fail because the format is ambiguous without an explicit pattern. Reference: Spark SQL date format patterns.

Question 4: B. `ROLLUP` produces hierarchical subtotals: totals by (year, quarter, month), by (year, quarter), by (year), and a grand total. `CUBE` would produce all possible combinations. Reference: Spark SQL GROUP BY extensions.

Question 5: B. `createOrReplaceGlobalTempView()` creates a view in the `global_temp` database that is accessible from any notebook attached to the same cluster. Regular temp views are scoped to the SparkSession. Reference: PySpark DataFrame API documentation.

Question 6: D. In PySpark, `col("properties").getItem("color")` or `element_at(col("properties"), "color")` retrieves a map value. In SQL, the bracket notation `properties['color']` works. Both approaches are valid. Reference: PySpark Column methods documentation.

Question 7: B. The `replaceWhere` option in Delta Lake write operations allows selectively overwriting only rows that match a specified predicate, leaving other data unchanged. Reference: Delta Lake write options documentation.

Question 8: C. `datediff()` returns an INTEGER representing the number of days between two dates. It does not return a fractional value or an interval type. Reference: Spark SQL datediff documentation. # Chapter 8: Advanced Transformations: Joins, Windows, and UDFs

Meridian Certification Press—Microsoft DP-750: Implementing Azure Databricks Study Guide 2026

1.82 Learning Objectives

After completing this chapter, you will be able to:

- Implement all join types in both PySpark and Spark SQL
- Apply window functions for ranking, aggregation, and analytics
- Create and use User-Defined Functions (UDFs) in Python and SQL
- Use higher-order functions to transform complex data types
- Implement pivot and unpivot operations
- Optimize join performance with broadcast joins and adaptive query execution

---

1.83 Join Operations

Joins combine rows from two or more tables based on a related column. Spark supports the same join types as traditional SQL databases.

1.83.1 Inner Join

Returns only rows with matching keys in both tables:

```
# PySpark inner join
orders_df = spark.table("analytics.silver.orders")
customers_df = spark.table("analytics.silver.customers")

result = orders_df.join(
    customers_df,
    orders_df.customer_id == customers_df.customer_id,
    "inner"
).select(
    orders_df.order_id,
    customers_df.name,
    orders_df.amount
)
```

```
-- SQL inner join
SELECT o.order_id, c.name, o.amount
FROM analytics.silver.orders o
INNER JOIN analytics.silver.customers c
    ON o.customer_id = c.customer_id;
```

1.83.2 Left Outer Join

Returns all rows from the left table and matching rows from the right:

```
# Left join - all orders, with customer info where available
result = orders_df.join(
    customers_df,
    orders_df.customer_id == customers_df.customer_id,
    "left"
)
```

```
SELECT o.order_id, o.amount, c.name, c.email
FROM analytics.silver.orders o
LEFT JOIN analytics.silver.customers c
    ON o.customer_id = c.customer_id;
```

1.83.3 Right Outer Join

Returns all rows from the right table and matching rows from the left:

```
result = orders_df.join(
    customers_df,
    orders_df.customer_id == customers_df.customer_id,
    "right"
)
```

1.83.4 Full Outer Join

Returns all rows from both tables, with nulls where no match exists:

```
result = orders_df.join(
    customers_df,
    orders_df.customer_id == customers_df.customer_id,
    "full"
)
```

```
SELECT o.order_id, o.amount, c.name
FROM analytics.silver.orders o
FULL OUTER JOIN analytics.silver.customers c
    ON o.customer_id = c.customer_id;
```

1.83.5 Cross Join

Returns the Cartesian product of both tables (every row paired with every other row):

```
# Cross join (use with caution - can produce very large results)
result = dates_df.crossJoin(products_df)
```

```
SELECT d.date, p.product_name
FROM analytics.dim_dates d
CROSS JOIN analytics.dim_products p;
```

1.83.6 Left Semi Join

Returns rows from the left table that have a match in the right table (like EXISTS):

```
# Semi join - orders from customers who have placed at least one return
result = orders_df.join(
    returns_df,
    orders_df.order_id == returns_df.order_id,
```

```
    "left_semi"
)
```

```
-- Equivalent SQL using EXISTS
SELECT o.*
FROM analytics.silver.orders o
WHERE EXISTS (
    SELECT 1 FROM analytics.silver.returns r
    WHERE r.order_id = o.order_id
);
```

1.83.7 Left Anti Join

Returns rows from the left table that do NOT have a match in the right table (like NOT EXISTS):

```
# Anti join - orders without any returns
result = orders_df.join(
    returns_df,
    orders_df.order_id == returns_df.order_id,
    "left_anti"
)
```

```
-- Equivalent SQL using NOT EXISTS
SELECT o.*
FROM analytics.silver.orders o
WHERE NOT EXISTS (
    SELECT 1 FROM analytics.silver.returns r
    WHERE r.order_id = o.order_id
);
```

> **Exam Tip:** Know all seven join types, especially **left semi** (rows with matches, like EXISTS) and **left anti** (rows without matches, like NOT EXISTS). These are frequently tested because they are less common in traditional SQL but very useful in data engineering. The PySpark join type strings are: `"inner"`, `"left"`, `"right"`, `"full"`, `"cross"`, `"left_semi"`, `"left_anti"`.

1.83.8 Join Column Handling

When joining on identically named columns, use the shorthand syntax to avoid duplicate columns:

```
# This creates duplicate customer_id columns
result = orders_df.join(customers_df,
    orders_df.customer_id == customers_df.customer_id)

# This avoids duplicate columns
result = orders_df.join(customers_df, "customer_id")

# Multiple join keys
result = orders_df.join(customers_df, ["customer_id", "region"])
```

1.84 Broadcast Joins

When one side of a join is small enough to fit in memory, a **broadcast join** distributes the smaller table to all worker nodes, avoiding an expensive shuffle:

```python
from pyspark.sql.functions import broadcast

# Explicitly broadcast the smaller table
result = orders_df.join(
    broadcast(customers_df),
    "customer_id"
)
```

```sql
-- SQL broadcast hint
SELECT /*+ BROADCAST(c) */ o.order_id, c.name, o.amount
FROM analytics.silver.orders o
JOIN analytics.silver.customers c
    ON o.customer_id = c.customer_id;
```

Broadcast join characteristics: - Default threshold: 10 MB (`spark.sql.autoBroadcastJoinThreshold`) - The smaller table is serialized and sent to all executors - Eliminates the shuffle stage on the larger table - Dramatically faster for joins with a small dimension table

```python
# Configure broadcast threshold
spark.conf.set("spark.sql.autoBroadcastJoinThreshold", "50m")  # 50 MB

# Disable auto-broadcast
spark.conf.set("spark.sql.autoBroadcastJoinThreshold", "-1")
```

> **Exam Tip:** Broadcast joins are the single most important join optimization concept for the exam. Know that Spark automatically broadcasts tables smaller than 10 MB, and that you can force broadcast with `broadcast()` or SQL hints. If a question asks how to optimize a join between a large fact table and a small dimension table, the answer is broadcast join.

1.85 Window Functions

Window functions perform calculations across a set of rows related to the current row, without collapsing rows like GROUP BY.

1.85.1 Window Specification

```python
from pyspark.sql.window import Window
from pyspark.sql.functions import row_number, rank, dense_rank, col

# Define a window specification
window_spec = Window.partitionBy("customer_id").orderBy(col("order_date").desc())
```

1.85.2 Ranking Functions

```python
from pyspark.sql.functions import row_number, rank, dense_rank, percent_rank, ntile

window_spec = Window.partitionBy("product_category").orderBy(col("revenue").desc())

df.select(
    col("product_name"),
    col("product_category"),
    col("revenue"),
    row_number().over(window_spec).alias("row_num"),
```

```
    rank().over(window_spec).alias("rank"),
    dense_rank().over(window_spec).alias("dense_rank"),
    percent_rank().over(window_spec).alias("pct_rank"),
    ntile(4).over(window_spec).alias("quartile")
)
```

```
-- SQL window ranking functions
SELECT
    product_name,
    product_category,
    revenue,
    ROW_NUMBER() OVER (
        PARTITION BY product_category ORDER BY revenue DESC
    ) AS row_num,
    RANK() OVER (
        PARTITION BY product_category ORDER BY revenue DESC
    ) AS rank,
    DENSE_RANK() OVER (
        PARTITION BY product_category ORDER BY revenue DESC
    ) AS dense_rank,
    PERCENT_RANK() OVER (
        PARTITION BY product_category ORDER BY revenue DESC
    ) AS pct_rank,
    NTILE(4) OVER (
        PARTITION BY product_category ORDER BY revenue DESC
    ) AS quartile
FROM analytics.silver.products;
```

Ranking function differences:

Function	Ties	Gaps	Example (values: 100, 90, 90, 80)
`ROW_NUMBER()`	No ties	N/A	1, 2, 3, 4
`RANK()`	Yes	Yes	1, 2, 2, 4
`DENSE_RANK()`	Yes	No	1, 2, 2, 3

Exam Tip: The difference between `ROW_NUMBER`, `RANK`, and `DENSE_RANK` is one of the most frequently tested window function topics. Remember: ROW_NUMBER always assigns unique sequential numbers. RANK leaves gaps after ties. DENSE_RANK has no gaps.

1.85.3 Aggregate Window Functions

```
from pyspark.sql.functions import sum, avg, count, min, max

# Running total
window_running = Window.partitionBy("customer_id") \
    .orderBy("order_date") \
    .rowsBetween(Window.unboundedPreceding, Window.currentRow)

df.withColumn("running_total", sum("amount").over(window_running))

# Moving average (last 7 rows)
window_moving = Window.partitionBy("product_id") \
    .orderBy("sale_date") \
    .rowsBetween(-6, Window.currentRow)

df.withColumn("moving_avg_7d", avg("quantity").over(window_moving))

# Total within partition (no ORDER BY = full partition)
```

```
window_total = Window.partitionBy("product_category")

df.withColumn("category_total", sum("revenue").over(window_total))
df.withColumn("pct_of_category",
    col("revenue") / sum("revenue").over(window_total) * 100)
```

```
-- SQL aggregate windows
SELECT
    customer_id,
    order_date,
    amount,
   ---Running total
    SUM(amount) OVER (
        PARTITION BY customer_id
        ORDER BY order_date
        ROWS BETWEEN UNBOUNDED PRECEDING AND CURRENT ROW
    ) AS running_total,
   ---Percentage of customer total
    amount / SUM(amount) OVER (PARTITION BY customer_id) * 100 AS pct_of_total,
   ---Moving average
    AVG(amount) OVER (
        PARTITION BY customer_id
        ORDER BY order_date
        ROWS BETWEEN 6 PRECEDING AND CURRENT ROW
    ) AS moving_avg_7
FROM analytics.silver.orders;
```

1.85.4 Offset Functions (LAG and LEAD)

```
from pyspark.sql.functions import lag, lead

window_spec = Window.partitionBy("customer_id").orderBy("order_date")

df.select(
    col("customer_id"),
    col("order_date"),
    col("amount"),
    lag("amount", 1).over(window_spec).alias("prev_amount"),
    lead("amount", 1).over(window_spec).alias("next_amount"),
    (col("amount") - lag("amount", 1).over(window_spec)).alias("change_from_prev"),
    lag("amount", 1, 0).over(window_spec).alias("prev_amount_default_zero")
)
```

```
-- SQL LAG and LEAD
SELECT
    customer_id,
    order_date,
    amount,
    LAG(amount, 1) OVER (
        PARTITION BY customer_id ORDER BY order_date
    ) AS prev_amount,
    LEAD(amount, 1) OVER (
        PARTITION BY customer_id ORDER BY order_date
    ) AS next_amount,
    amount - LAG(amount, 1) OVER (
        PARTITION BY customer_id ORDER BY order_date
    ) AS change_from_prev,
    FIRST_VALUE(amount) OVER (
```

```
        PARTITION BY customer_id ORDER BY order_date
    ) AS first_order_amount,
    LAST_VALUE(amount) OVER (
        PARTITION BY customer_id
        ORDER BY order_date
        ROWS BETWEEN UNBOUNDED PRECEDING AND UNBOUNDED FOLLOWING
    ) AS last_order_amount
FROM analytics.silver.orders;
```

> **Exam Tip:** `LAG()` looks backward (previous rows); `LEAD()` looks forward (next rows). Both accept an optional default value as the third argument. `LAST_VALUE` requires an explicit frame specification (`ROWS BETWEEN UNBOUNDED PRECEDING AND UNBOUNDED FOLLOWING`) to work correctly; otherwise it only considers rows up to the current row.

1.85.5 Window Frame Specifications

Window frames define which rows are included in the calculation relative to the current row:

```
from pyspark.sql.window import Window

# ROWS frame - based on physical row position
Window.partitionBy("id").orderBy("date") \
    .rowsBetween(Window.unboundedPreceding, Window.currentRow)

# RANGE frame - based on logical value range
Window.partitionBy("id").orderBy("date") \
    .rangeBetween(Window.unboundedPreceding, Window.currentRow)

# Common frame boundaries:
# Window.unboundedPreceding  = from the first row of the partition
# Window.currentRow          = the current row
# Window.unboundedFollowing  = to the last row of the partition
# -N                         = N rows before current
# N                          = N rows after current
```

1.86 Pivot and Unpivot

1.86.1 Pivot (Rows to Columns)

```
# Pivot: convert row values into columns
pivoted = (df
    .groupBy("customer_id")
    .pivot("product_category", ["Electronics", "Clothing", "Food"])
    .agg(sum("amount"))
)
```

```
-- SQL PIVOT
SELECT * FROM (
    SELECT customer_id, product_category, amount
    FROM analytics.silver.orders
)
PIVOT (
    SUM(amount) FOR product_category IN (
        'Electronics', 'Clothing', 'Food'
```

```
    )
);
```

1.86.2 Unpivot (Columns to Rows)

```
-- SQL UNPIVOT
SELECT customer_id, category, total_amount
FROM analytics.gold.customer_category_totals
UNPIVOT (
    total_amount FOR category IN (
        Electronics, Clothing, Food
    )
);
```

```
# PySpark unpivot using stack()
from pyspark.sql.functions import expr

unpivoted = df.select(
    "customer_id",
    expr("""
        STACK(3,
            'Electronics', Electronics,
            'Clothing', Clothing,
            'Food', Food
        ) AS (category, total_amount)
    """)
).filter(col("total_amount").isNotNull())
```

Exam Tip: Pivot transforms row values into column headers (wide format). Unpivot transforms column headers back into row values (long format). The exam may ask you to identify which operation converts data between these two formats.

1.87 User-Defined Functions (UDFs)

1.87.1 Python UDFs

```
from pyspark.sql.functions import udf
from pyspark.sql.types import StringType, DoubleType

# Define a Python UDF
@udf(returnType=StringType())
def classify_amount(amount):
    if amount is None:
        return "unknown"
    elif amount > 1000:
        return "high"
    elif amount > 100:
        return "medium"
    else:
        return "low"

# Use the UDF
df.withColumn("amount_class", classify_amount(col("amount")))
```

```python
# Alternative: register UDF without decorator
def calculate_tax(amount, rate):
    if amount is None or rate is None:
        return None
    return round(float(amount) * float(rate), 2)

tax_udf = udf(calculate_tax, DoubleType())
df.withColumn("tax", tax_udf(col("amount"), col("tax_rate")))
```

1.87.2 Pandas UDFs (Vectorized UDFs)

Pandas UDFs are significantly faster than regular Python UDFs because they process data in vectorized batches using Apache Arrow:

```python
import pandas as pd
from pyspark.sql.functions import pandas_udf
from pyspark.sql.types import DoubleType

# Scalar Pandas UDF (one-to-one mapping)
@pandas_udf(DoubleType())
def normalize_amount(amount: pd.Series) -> pd.Series:
    return (amount - amount.mean()) / amount.std()

df.withColumn("normalized_amount", normalize_amount(col("amount")))

# Grouped Map Pandas UDF
@pandas_udf("customer_id long, amount double, z_score double",
            PandasUDFType.GROUPED_MAP)
def compute_z_scores(pdf: pd.DataFrame) -> pd.DataFrame:
    mean = pdf["amount"].mean()
    std = pdf["amount"].std()
    pdf["z_score"] = (pdf["amount"] - mean) / std
    return pdf[["customer_id", "amount", "z_score"]]

df.groupBy("product_category").apply(compute_z_scores)
```

> **Exam Tip:** Pandas UDFs (vectorized UDFs) are **much faster** than regular Python UDFs because they use Apache Arrow for serialization and process data in batches rather than row by row. When a question asks about UDF performance optimization, Pandas UDFs are usually the answer.

1.87.3 SQL UDFs

```sql
-- Create a SQL UDF
CREATE OR REPLACE FUNCTION analytics.functions.classify_amount(amount DECIMAL(10,2))
RETURNS STRING
RETURN CASE
    WHEN amount > 1000 THEN 'high'
    WHEN amount > 100 THEN 'medium'
    ELSE 'low'
END;

-- Use the SQL UDF
SELECT
    order_id,
    amount,
    analytics.functions.classify_amount(amount) AS amount_class
FROM analytics.silver.orders;
```

```sql
-- Create a SQL table-valued function
CREATE OR REPLACE FUNCTION analytics.functions.get_top_customers(n INT)
RETURNS TABLE (customer_id BIGINT, total_spend DECIMAL(12,2))
RETURN
    SELECT customer_id, SUM(amount) AS total_spend
    FROM analytics.silver.orders
    GROUP BY customer_id
    ORDER BY total_spend DESC
    LIMIT n;

-- Use the table-valued function
SELECT * FROM analytics.functions.get_top_customers(10);
```

1.87.4 UDF Performance Comparison

UDF Type	Performance	Use Case
SQL UDF	Fastest (optimized by Catalyst)	Simple expressions, reusable logic
Pandas UDF	Fast (vectorized, Arrow)	Complex Python logic, ML inference
Python UDF	Slow (row-by-row serialization)	Last resort for complex custom logic

---

1.88 Higher-Order Functions

Higher-order functions operate on complex types (arrays, maps) without needing to explode them:

1.88.1 TRANSFORM

Apply a function to each element of an array:

```sql
-- Double every element in an array
SELECT
    order_id,
    items,
    TRANSFORM(items, x -> x * 2) AS doubled_items
FROM analytics.silver.orders;

-- Extract a field from an array of structs
SELECT
    order_id,
    TRANSFORM(line_items, item -> item.product_name) AS product_names
FROM analytics.silver.orders;
```

```python
from pyspark.sql.functions import transform, col

df.withColumn("doubled", transform(col("items"), lambda x: x * 2))
```

1.88.2 FILTER

Filter elements of an array based on a condition:

```
-- Keep only items above a threshold
SELECT
    order_id,
    items,
    FILTER(items, x -> x > 100) AS high_value_items
FROM analytics.silver.orders;
```

```
from pyspark.sql.functions import filter as array_filter

df.withColumn("high_value",
    array_filter(col("prices"), lambda x: x > 100))
```

1.88.3 AGGREGATE (REDUCE)

Reduce an array to a single value:

```
-- Sum all elements in an array
SELECT
    order_id,
    line_amounts,
    AGGREGATE(line_amounts, 0D, (acc, x) -> acc + x) AS total
FROM analytics.silver.orders;

-- Concatenate array elements
SELECT
    order_id,
    AGGREGATE(tags, '', (acc, x) -> CONCAT(acc, IF(acc = '', '', ', '), x)) AS tag_string
FROM analytics.silver.orders;
```

1.88.4 EXISTS and FORALL

```
-- Check if any element satisfies a condition
SELECT order_id
FROM analytics.silver.orders
WHERE EXISTS(line_amounts, x -> x > 1000);

-- Check if all elements satisfy a condition
SELECT order_id
FROM analytics.silver.orders
WHERE FORALL(line_amounts, x -> x > 0);
```

> **Exam Tip:** Higher-order functions (TRANSFORM, FILTER, AGGREGATE, EXISTS) are a modern alternative to EXPLODE + operation + COLLECT. They are more efficient because they avoid the expensive explode-and-recollect pattern. Know the syntax and use cases for each.

1.89 Set Operations

```
# Union (combines rows, keeps duplicates)
df1.union(df2)

# Union by name (matches columns by name, not position)
df1.unionByName(df2, allowMissingColumns=True)
```

```
# Intersect (rows in both)
df1.intersect(df2)

# Except (rows in df1 but not df2)
df1.exceptAll(df2)
```

```
-- SQL set operations
SELECT * FROM table1
UNION ALL
SELECT * FROM table2;

SELECT * FROM table1
INTERSECT
SELECT * FROM table2;

SELECT * FROM table1
EXCEPT
SELECT * FROM table2;
```

Exam Tip: `UNION` removes duplicates; `UNION ALL` keeps them. `union()` in PySpark is equivalent to SQL `UNION ALL` (keeps duplicates). Use `df.union(df2).distinct()` for SQL `UNION` behavior. Also know that `unionByName` matches by column name, not position—essential when schemas differ in column order.

1.90 Common Table Expressions (CTEs)

```
-- SQL CTEs for readable multi-step transformations
WITH customer_totals AS (
    SELECT
        customer_id,
        SUM(amount) AS total_spend,
        COUNT(*) AS order_count
    FROM analytics.silver.orders
    WHERE status = 'COMPLETED'
    GROUP BY customer_id
),
customer_segments AS (
    SELECT
        customer_id,
        total_spend,
        order_count,
        CASE
            WHEN total_spend > 10000 THEN 'VIP'
            WHEN total_spend > 1000 THEN 'Regular'
            ELSE 'Occasional'
        END AS segment
    FROM customer_totals
)
SELECT
    c.name,
    c.email,
    cs.segment,
    cs.total_spend,
    cs.order_count
FROM customer_segments cs
```

```
JOIN analytics.silver.customers c ON cs.customer_id = c.customer_id
ORDER BY cs.total_spend DESC;
```

1.91 Chapter Summary

In this chapter, you learned:

- Spark supports seven join types: **inner, left, right, full, cross, left semi, left anti**
- **Broadcast joins** optimize large-small table joins by distributing the smaller table to all workers
- **Window functions** enable ranking (ROW_NUMBER, RANK, DENSE_RANK), aggregation (running totals, moving averages), and offset (LAG, LEAD) calculations
- **Pivot** transforms rows to columns; **unpivot** transforms columns to rows
- **UDFs** come in three flavors: Python (slow), Pandas/vectorized (fast), and SQL (fastest)
- **Higher-order functions** (TRANSFORM, FILTER, AGGREGATE) operate on arrays without exploding
- **Set operations** (UNION, INTERSECT, EXCEPT) combine result sets; PySpark `union()` is equivalent to SQL `UNION ALL`

1.92 Practice Questions

Question 1: Which join type returns rows from the left table that have NO match in the right table?

A. Left semi join B. Left anti join C. Left outer join D. Full outer join

Question 2: A fact table has 500 million rows and a dimension table has 5,000 rows. Which optimization should be applied to the join?

A. Sort-merge join B. Broadcast join on the dimension table C. Hash join with bucketing D. Nested loop join

Question 3: Given values 100, 90, 90, 80, what does `RANK()` return for each row when ordering by value DESC?

A. 1, 2, 3, 4 B. 1, 2, 2, 4 C. 1, 2, 2, 3 D. 1, 2, 3, 3

Question 4: Which window function retrieves the value from the previous row?

A. `LEAD()` B. `LAG()` C. `FIRST_VALUE()` D. `NTH_VALUE()`

Question 5: A data engineer needs to apply a complex Python function to a large DataFrame. Which UDF type provides the best performance?

A. Regular Python UDF B. Pandas UDF (vectorized) C. SQL UDF D. Scala UDF

Question 6: Which higher-order function applies a transformation to each element of an array?

A. `FILTER` B. `TRANSFORM` C. `AGGREGATE` D. `EXISTS`

Question 7: In PySpark, `df1.union(df2)` is equivalent to which SQL operation?

A. `UNION` (removes duplicates) B. `UNION ALL` (keeps duplicates) C. `INTERSECT` D. `EXCEPT`

Question 8: A window function needs to calculate the average of the current row and the 6 preceding rows. Which frame specification is correct?

A. `ROWS BETWEEN UNBOUNDED PRECEDING AND CURRENT ROW` B. `ROWS BETWEEN 6 PRECEDING AND CURRENT ROW` C. `ROWS BETWEEN CURRENT ROW AND 6 FOLLOWING` D. `ROWS BETWEEN 6 PRECEDING AND 6 FOLLOWING`

Question 9: Which SQL clause converts row values in a column into separate column headers?

A. `UNPIVOT` B. `PIVOT` C. `LATERAL VIEW` D. `TRANSFORM`

Question 10: What is the default broadcast join threshold in Spark?

A. 1 MB B. 10 MB C. 100 MB D. 1 GB

1.93 Answer Explanations

Question 1: B. Left anti join returns rows from the left table that do NOT have a match in the right table. It is equivalent to a `NOT EXISTS` subquery. Left semi join returns rows that DO have a match. Reference: PySpark join documentation.

Question 2: B. When joining a large fact table with a small dimension table, broadcasting the dimension table to all workers avoids an expensive shuffle of the fact table. At 5,000 rows, the dimension table is well within the broadcast threshold. Reference: Spark broadcast join documentation.

Question 3: B. `RANK()` assigns the same rank to tied values and leaves a gap after the tie. Values 100=1, 90=2, 90=2 (tied), 80=4 (skips 3). `DENSE_RANK()` would produce 1, 2, 2, 3 (no gap). Reference: Spark SQL window function documentation.

Question 4: B. `LAG()` retrieves values from previous (preceding) rows. `LEAD()` retrieves values from following (subsequent) rows. The first argument is the column, the second is the offset (default 1), and the optional third is a default value. Reference: Spark SQL LAG documentation.

Question 5: B. Pandas UDFs (vectorized UDFs) provide the best performance for complex Python logic because they use Apache Arrow for efficient serialization and process data in batches. SQL UDFs are fastest but limited to SQL expressions. Reference: Databricks UDF performance guide.

Question 6: B. `TRANSFORM` applies a lambda function to each element of an array, returning a new array of the same size. `FILTER` keeps elements matching a predicate. `AGGREGATE` reduces an array to a single value. Reference: Spark SQL higher-order functions.

Question 7: B. PySpark's `union()` keeps all rows including duplicates, which is equivalent to SQL `UNION ALL`. To achieve SQL `UNION` behavior (removing duplicates), use `df1.union(df2).distinct()`. Reference: PySpark DataFrame union documentation.

Question 8: B. `ROWS BETWEEN 6 PRECEDING AND CURRENT ROW` includes the current row plus the 6 immediately preceding rows, giving a 7-row window for the moving average. Reference: Spark SQL window frame specification.

Question 9: B. `PIVOT` converts distinct values from a column into separate columns, effectively rotating rows into columns. `UNPIVOT` does the reverse. Reference: Spark SQL PIVOT documentation.

Question 10: B. The default `spark.sql.autoBroadcastJoinThreshold` is 10 MB (10485760 bytes). Tables smaller than this threshold are automatically broadcast during joins. Set to -1 to disable auto-broadcast. Reference: Spark configuration documentation. # Chapter 9: Structured Streaming

Meridian Certification Press—Microsoft DP-750: Implementing Azure Databricks Study Guide 2026

1.94 Learning Objectives

After completing this chapter, you will be able to:

- Explain the Structured Streaming programming model and its guarantees
- Configure streaming sources and sinks for production pipelines
- Implement trigger modes for different processing requirements
- Apply watermarks for handling late-arriving data
- Use stateful operations including windowed aggregations
- Monitor and troubleshoot streaming queries
- Manage checkpoints for fault tolerance

1.95 Introduction to Structured Streaming

Structured Streaming is the Apache Spark engine for processing real-time data streams. It treats a data stream as an unbounded table that grows continuously as new data arrives. You write streaming queries using the same DataFrame and SQL APIs used for batch processing.

1.95.1 The Unbounded Table Model

```
Time 1:   | Row 1 | Row 2 | Row 3 |
Time 2:   | Row 1 | Row 2 | Row 3 | Row 4 | Row 5 |
Time 3:   | Row 1 | Row 2 | Row 3 | Row 4 | Row 5 | Row 6 | Row 7 |
```

Each trigger interval, Spark: 1. Checks for new data in the source 2. Processes the new data incrementally 3. Updates the result table 4. Writes output to the sink

1.95.2 Key Guarantees

- **Exactly-once semantics:** Each input record is processed exactly once, even in the event of failures
- **Fault tolerance:** Checkpoints and write-ahead logs enable recovery from failures without data loss or duplication
- **Consistency:** Output is always consistent with the input at a point in time

> **Exam Tip:** Structured Streaming provides **exactly-once** processing guarantees when used with checkpointing and a supported sink (like Delta Lake). This is a commonly tested concept. The combination of checkpoints (tracking progress) and Delta Lake's transaction log (idempotent writes) ensures no data loss or duplication.

1.96 Streaming Sources

1.96.1 Delta Lake as a Streaming Source

```
# Read a Delta table as a stream
stream_df = (spark.readStream
    .format("delta")
    .table("analytics.bronze.events"))

# With rate limiting
stream_df = (spark.readStream
    .format("delta")
    .option("maxFilesPerTrigger", 100)
    .option("maxBytesPerTrigger", "10g")
    .table("analytics.bronze.events"))

# Read only changes (Change Data Feed)
stream_df = (spark.readStream
    .format("delta")
    .option("readChangeFeed", "true")
    .option("startingVersion", 0)
    .table("analytics.silver.customers"))
```

1.96.2 Auto Loader (Cloud Files) as Source

```
# Auto Loader streaming source (covered in Chapter 6)
stream_df = (spark.readStream
    .format("cloudFiles")
    .option("cloudFiles.format", "json")
    .option("cloudFiles.schemaLocation", "/checkpoints/schema/")
    .load("/Volumes/raw/events/"))
```

1.96.3 Apache Kafka as Source

```
# Read from Kafka
stream_df = (spark.readStream
    .format("kafka")
    .option("kafka.bootstrap.servers", "broker1:9092,broker2:9092")
    .option("subscribe", "events-topic")
    .option("startingOffsets", "latest")
    .load())

# Parse Kafka value (usually JSON)
from pyspark.sql.functions import from_json, col
from pyspark.sql.types import *

event_schema = StructType([
    StructField("event_id", StringType()),
    StructField("event_type", StringType()),
    StructField("user_id", LongType()),
    StructField("timestamp", TimestampType()),
    StructField("payload", StringType())
])

parsed_df = (stream_df
    .select(from_json(col("value").cast("string"), event_schema).alias("data"))
    .select("data.*"))
```

1.96.4 Rate Source (Testing)

```
# Generate synthetic data for testing
test_df = (spark.readStream
    .format("rate")
    .option("rowsPerSecond", 100)
    .load())
# Produces: timestamp (TIMESTAMP), value (LONG)
```

Exam Tip: Know the common streaming sources: **Delta Lake** (table-to-table streaming), **Auto Loader/cloudFiles** (file ingestion), **Kafka** (message queue), and **rate** (testing). Delta Lake is the most commonly tested source on the DP-750.

1.97 Streaming Sinks

1.97.1 Delta Lake Sink

```
# Write stream to a Delta table
(stream_df.writeStream
    .format("delta")
    .outputMode("append")
    .option("checkpointLocation", "/checkpoints/events_silver/")
    .toTable("analytics.silver.events"))
```

1.97.2 Kafka Sink

```
# Write stream to Kafka
(stream_df
    .select(col("event_id").cast("string").alias("key"),
            to_json(struct("*")).alias("value"))
    .writeStream
    .format("kafka")
    .option("kafka.bootstrap.servers", "broker1:9092")
    .option("topic", "processed-events")
    .option("checkpointLocation", "/checkpoints/kafka_out/")
    .start())
```

1.97.3 Console Sink (Debugging)

```
# Write to console for debugging (not for production)
(stream_df.writeStream
    .format("console")
    .outputMode("append")
    .option("truncate", False)
    .start())
```

1.97.4 Memory Sink (Testing)

```
# Write to in-memory table for testing
(stream_df.writeStream
    .format("memory")
    .queryName("test_events")
    .outputMode("complete")
    .start())

# Query the in-memory table
spark.sql("SELECT * FROM test_events")
```

1.98 Output Modes

Structured Streaming supports three output modes that determine which results are written to the sink:

1.98.1 Append Mode (Default)

Only new rows added to the result table since the last trigger are written to the sink. Used for queries that do not contain aggregations, or aggregations with watermarks.

```
(stream_df.writeStream
    .outputMode("append")
    .format("delta")
    .option("checkpointLocation", "/checkpoints/append/")
    .toTable("analytics.silver.events"))
```

1.98.2 Complete Mode

The entire result table is written to the sink after every trigger. Used for aggregation queries where you want to see the full result.

```
(stream_df
    .groupBy("event_type")
    .count()
    .writeStream
    .outputMode("complete")
    .format("delta")
    .option("checkpointLocation", "/checkpoints/complete/")
    .toTable("analytics.gold.event_counts"))
```

1.98.3 Update Mode

Only rows that have changed since the last trigger are written to the sink. More efficient than complete mode for aggregation queries.

```
(stream_df
    .groupBy("event_type")
    .count()
    .writeStream
    .outputMode("update")
    .format("delta")
    .option("checkpointLocation", "/checkpoints/update/")
    .toTable("analytics.gold.event_counts"))
```

Output Mode	Writes	Supported Operations	Common Use
Append	New rows only	No aggregations (or with watermark)	Event logs, raw data
Complete	Full result table	Aggregations	Small result sets, dashboards
Update	Changed rows only	Aggregations	Efficient aggregation updates

> **Exam Tip:** This is a heavily tested topic. Remember: **append** = new rows only (default, no aggregation), **complete** = entire result table rewritten (aggregations), **update** = only changed rows (aggregations). A streaming query with `groupBy().count()` without a watermark requires complete or update mode, not append.

1.99 Trigger Modes

Triggers control when the streaming query processes new data:

1.99.1 Default (Micro-Batch)

```
# Processes the next micro-batch as soon as the previous one completes
(stream_df.writeStream
    .format("delta")
    .option("checkpointLocation", "/checkpoints/default/")
    .start())
```

1.99.2 Fixed Interval

```
# Process a micro-batch every 30 seconds
(stream_df.writeStream
    .trigger(processingTime="30 seconds")
    .format("delta")
    .option("checkpointLocation", "/checkpoints/interval/")
    .start())
```

1.99.3 Available Now

```
# Process all available data, then stop (batch-like behavior)
(stream_df.writeStream
    .trigger(availableNow=True)
    .format("delta")
    .option("checkpointLocation", "/checkpoints/avail/")
    .start())
```

1.99.4 Once (Legacy)

```
# Process one micro-batch, then stop
(stream_df.writeStream
    .trigger(once=True)
    .format("delta")
    .option("checkpointLocation", "/checkpoints/once/")
    .start())
```

Trigger	Behavior	Use Case
Default	Continuous micro-batches	Low-latency requirements
`processingTime`	Fixed interval batches	Controlled resource usage
`availableNow`	All available data, then stop	Scheduled batch jobs
`once` (legacy)	Single micro-batch, then stop	Simple batch, legacy

> **Exam Tip:** `trigger(availableNow=True)` is the recommended replacement for `trigger(once=True)`. The key difference: `availableNow` processes all available data across multiple efficient micro-batches, while `once` processes everything in a single micro-batch (which can cause OOM errors on large datasets).

1.100 Watermarks and Late Data

1.100.1 The Late Data Problem

In real-world streaming, events often arrive out of order or late. A watermark defines how long the system should wait for late-arriving data before considering a time window "closed."

1.100.2 Defining Watermarks

```
from pyspark.sql.functions import window, col

# Define a watermark of 10 minutes on the event_time column
windowed_counts = (stream_df
    .withWatermark("event_time", "10 minutes")
    .groupBy(
```

```
        window("event_time", "5 minutes"),
        "event_type"
    )
    .count())

(windowed_counts.writeStream
    .outputMode("append")  # Watermark enables append mode with aggregation
    .format("delta")
    .option("checkpointLocation", "/checkpoints/windowed/")
    .toTable("analytics.gold.event_window_counts"))
```

How watermarks work:

1. The watermark tracks the maximum event time seen so far
2. The watermark threshold = max event time - watermark delay
3. Events with event time older than the watermark threshold are considered "too late" and may be dropped
4. Windows are finalized and emitted in append mode only after the watermark passes their end time

```
Max event time seen:    12:30
Watermark delay:        10 minutes
Watermark threshold:    12:20

Events before 12:20 → may be dropped
Window [12:00, 12:05] → finalized (end time 12:05 < 12:20)
Window [12:15, 12:20] → still open (end time 12:20 = threshold)
Window [12:25, 12:30] → still open (end time 12:30 > 12:20)
```

> **Exam Tip:** Watermarks serve two critical purposes: (1) they allow **append mode with aggregations** by defining when windows are finalized, and (2) they **bound the state** that Spark must maintain, preventing unbounded state growth. Without a watermark, Spark must keep all partial aggregation state forever. This is one of the most important streaming concepts for the exam.

1.101 Windowed Aggregations

1.101.1 Tumbling Windows (Non-Overlapping)

```python
from pyspark.sql.functions import window

# 5-minute tumbling windows
result = (stream_df
    .withWatermark("event_time", "10 minutes")
    .groupBy(
        window("event_time", "5 minutes"),
        "event_type"
    )
    .agg(
        count("*").alias("event_count"),
        avg("response_time").alias("avg_response")
    ))
```

```sql
-- SQL tumbling window
SELECT
    window.start,
    window.end,
    event_type,
    COUNT(*) AS event_count,
```

```
    AVG(response_time) AS avg_response
FROM events_stream
GROUP BY
    WINDOW(event_time, '5 minutes'),
    event_type;
```

1.101.2 Sliding Windows (Overlapping)

```
# 10-minute windows sliding every 5 minutes
result = (stream_df
    .withWatermark("event_time", "10 minutes")
    .groupBy(
        window("event_time", "10 minutes", "5 minutes"),
        "event_type"
    )
    .count())
```

1.101.3 Session Windows

```
# Session windows with 5-minute gap
result = (stream_df
    .withWatermark("event_time", "10 minutes")
    .groupBy(
        session_window("event_time", "5 minutes"),
        "user_id"
    )
    .count())
```

Window Type	Parameters	Overlap	Use Case
Tumbling	`window(col, duration)`	No	Fixed-period metrics
Sliding	`window(col, duration, slide )`	Yes	Moving averages
Session	`session_window(col, gap)`	No	User session analysis

Exam Tip: Tumbling windows have no overlap (each event belongs to exactly one window). Sliding windows overlap when the slide interval is less than the window duration (events may belong to multiple windows). Session windows are dynamic and based on activity gaps.

1.102 Stream-Stream Joins

```
# Join two streams with a watermark
impressions = (spark.readStream
    .format("delta")
    .table("analytics.bronze.ad_impressions")
    .withWatermark("impression_time", "2 hours"))

clicks = (spark.readStream
    .format("delta")
    .table("analytics.bronze.ad_clicks")
    .withWatermark("click_time", "3 hours"))
```

```
# Inner join with time constraint
matched = impressions.join(
    clicks,
    (impressions.ad_id == clicks.ad_id) &
    (clicks.click_time >= impressions.impression_time) &
    (clicks.click_time <= impressions.impression_time + expr("INTERVAL 1 HOUR")),
    "inner"
)
```

Stream-stream join requirements: - Both sides must have watermarks defined - The join condition must include a time constraint - Supported join types: inner, left outer (with watermark on right), right outer (with watermark on left)

1.103 Checkpoints and Fault Tolerance

1.103.1 Checkpoint Location

Every streaming query requires a checkpoint location to store progress information:

```
(stream_df.writeStream
    .format("delta")
    .option("checkpointLocation", "/checkpoints/my_query/")
    .toTable("analytics.silver.events"))
```

The checkpoint stores: - **Offsets:** Which data has been read from the source - **State:** Aggregation state for stateful operations - **Commit log:** Which micro-batches have been committed to the sink

1.103.2 Checkpoint Rules

1. Each streaming query must have a **unique** checkpoint location
2. **Never share** a checkpoint location between different queries
3. **Never delete** a checkpoint unless you want to reprocess all data
4. The checkpoint location should be on **reliable cloud storage** (ADLS Gen2), not local disk
5. Changing the query logic may require a **new checkpoint** (breaking changes)

> **Exam Tip:** Checkpoint management is critical for production streaming. Know that: (1) each query needs a unique checkpoint, (2) deleting a checkpoint causes full reprocessing, (3) some query changes are incompatible with existing checkpoints (adding/removing columns in aggregations, changing window duration). Non-breaking changes include adding filters or map operations.

1.104 Monitoring Streaming Queries

1.104.1 Query Progress

```
# Get active streaming queries
for q in spark.streams.active:
    print(f"Query: {q.name}, Status: {q.status}, Progress: {q.lastProgress}")

# Get detailed progress for a specific query
query = stream_df.writeStream.format("delta") \
    .option("checkpointLocation", "/checkpoints/events/") \
    .queryName("events_pipeline") \
```

```
    .toTable("analytics.silver.events")

# Check progress
print(query.lastProgress)
print(query.status)
```

1.104.2 Key Metrics

Metric	Description	Warning Sign
`inputRowsPerSecond`	Rows arriving per second	Consistently increasing
`processedRowsPerSecond`	Rows processed per second	Lower than input rate
`batchDuration`	Time to process a micro-batch	Exceeding trigger interval
`stateOperator.numRowsTotal`	Total rows in state store	Unbounded growth

1.104.3 Stopping a Stream

```
# Stop a specific query
query.stop()

# Stop all streaming queries
for q in spark.streams.active:
    q.stop()

# Await termination (blocks until query stops)
query.awaitTermination()
query.awaitTermination(timeout=300)  # 5 minute timeout
```

1.105 Change Data Feed (CDF)

Delta Lake's Change Data Feed captures row-level changes (inserts, updates, deletes):

```
-- Enable Change Data Feed on a table
ALTER TABLE analytics.silver.customers
SET TBLPROPERTIES ('delta.enableChangeDataFeed' = 'true');
```

```
# Read changes as a stream
changes = (spark.readStream
    .format("delta")
    .option("readChangeFeed", "true")
    .option("startingVersion", 0)
    .table("analytics.silver.customers"))

# The changes include special columns:
# _change_type: insert, update_preimage, update_postimage, delete
# _commit_version: the Delta version
# _commit_timestamp: when the change occurred

# Process only inserts and updates
new_and_updated = changes.filter(
    col("_change_type").isin("insert", "update_postimage")
)
```

Exam Tip: Change Data Feed (CDF) must be explicitly enabled with the `delta.enableChangeDataFeed` table property. It adds three metadata columns: `_change_type`, `_commit_version`, and `_commit_timestamp`. For updates, CDF produces two rows: `update_preimage` (before) and `update_postimage` (after).

1.106 Chapter Summary

In this chapter, you learned:

- Structured Streaming treats data streams as **unbounded tables** with exactly-once guarantees
- Common sources include **Delta Lake, Auto Loader, Kafka**, and rate (testing)
- Three output modes: **append** (new rows), **complete** (full result), **update** (changed rows)
- Trigger modes control processing frequency: **default, processingTime, availableNow, once**
- **Watermarks** handle late data and enable append-mode aggregations by bounding state
- **Window types**: tumbling (non-overlapping), sliding (overlapping), session (gap-based)
- **Checkpoints** enable fault tolerance; each query needs a unique checkpoint location
- **Change Data Feed** captures row-level changes for downstream streaming consumption

---

1.107 Practice Questions

Question 1: Which output mode writes only new rows to the sink and is the default for non-aggregation queries?

A. Complete B. Update C. Append D. Overwrite

Question 2: A streaming query aggregates event counts by event type. The query has no watermark defined. Which output modes are supported?

A. Append and Complete B. Complete and Update C. Only Append D. All three modes

Question 3: What is the purpose of a watermark in Structured Streaming?

A. To encrypt data in transit B. To define how long to wait for late-arriving data and bound state size C. To set the trigger interval for micro-batch processing D. To partition streaming data by time

Question 4: A data engineer changes the checkpoint location of a streaming query to a new, empty directory. What happens?

A. The query resumes from where it left off B. The query reprocesses all data from the beginning C. The query fails with an error D. The query creates a new checkpoint and skips existing data

Question 5: Which trigger mode processes all available data across multiple micro-batches and then stops?

A. `trigger(once=True)` B. `trigger(availableNow=True)` C. `trigger(processingTime="0 seconds")` D. Default trigger

Question 6: What does the `_change_type` column in Change Data Feed contain for a row that was updated?

A. Only `update` B. `update_preimage` and `update_postimage` (two separate rows) C. `modified` D. `update_before` and `update_after`

Question 7: A streaming query uses a watermark of "10 minutes" on the `event_time` column. The maximum event time seen so far is 14:30. Which events may be dropped?

A. Events with event_time before 14:20 B. Events with event_time before 14:30 C. Events with event_time before 14:40 D. No events are dropped

Question 8: Which window type creates windows that overlap, where a single event may belong to multiple windows?

A. Tumbling window B. Sliding window C. Session window D. Hopping window

Question 9: What happens if two streaming queries share the same checkpoint location?

A. Both queries run correctly with shared state B. The queries automatically coordinate via locking C. Data corruption or unexpected behavior occurs D. The second query fails to start with a clear error

Question 10: Which Delta Lake table property must be enabled to use Change Data Feed?

A. `delta.enableCDC` B. `delta.enableChangeDataFeed` C. `delta.changeTracking` D. `delta.trackChanges`

1.108 Answer Explanations

Question 1: C. Append mode writes only new rows to the sink and is the default output mode. It works with non-aggregation queries and aggregation queries that have watermarks defined. Reference: Structured Streaming output modes documentation.

Question 2: B. Without a watermark, aggregation queries cannot use append mode (because the system does not know when to finalize results). Complete and update modes are supported because they rewrite or update results on every trigger. Reference: Structured Streaming aggregation output modes.

Question 3: B. Watermarks define the threshold for late-arriving data and allow Spark to bound the amount of state it must maintain. Events older than the watermark threshold may be dropped, and windows past the watermark are finalized for append output. Reference: Structured Streaming watermark documentation.

Question 4: B. Changing to a new, empty checkpoint location causes the query to lose all progress tracking. It will reprocess all data from the source from the beginning, as if it were a brand new query. Reference: Structured Streaming checkpoint documentation.

Question 5: B. `trigger(availableNow=True)` processes all available data across multiple efficient micro-batches and then stops. `trigger(once=True)` processes everything in a single micro-batch, which is less efficient. Reference: Structured Streaming trigger modes.

Question 6: B. For updates, Change Data Feed produces two rows: `update_preimage` (the row before the update) and `update_postimage` (the row after the update). Inserts produce `insert` and deletes produce `delete`. Reference: Delta Lake Change Data Feed documentation.

Question 7: A. The watermark threshold is calculated as max event time minus watermark delay: 14:30 - 10 minutes = 14:20. Events with event_time before 14:20 may be dropped as late data. Reference: Structured Streaming watermark calculation.

Question 8: B. Sliding windows overlap when the slide interval is less than the window duration. For example, a 10-minute window sliding every 5 minutes means each event belongs to two windows. Tumbling windows do not overlap. Reference: Structured Streaming window operations.

Question 9: C. Sharing a checkpoint location between two different streaming queries leads to data corruption or unexpected behavior. Each query must have its own unique checkpoint location. Reference: Structured Streaming checkpoint best practices.

Question 10: B. The table property `delta.enableChangeDataFeed` must be set to `true` to enable Change Data Feed. This can be set at table creation or altered on an existing table. Reference: Delta Lake Change Data Feed setup documentation. # Chapter 10: Delta Live Tables (DLT) Pipelines

Meridian Certification Press—Microsoft DP-750: Implementing Azure Databricks Study Guide 2026

1.109 Learning Objectives

After completing this chapter, you will be able to:

- Explain the Delta Live Tables (DLT) programming model and its advantages
- Create DLT pipelines using Python and SQL
- Implement data quality expectations with `@dlt.expect`
- Build medallion architecture pipelines with DLT
- Configure pipeline settings including development and production modes
- Manage DLT pipeline lifecycle and dependencies
- Troubleshoot common DLT issues using the event log

1.110 Introduction to Delta Live Tables

Delta Live Tables (DLT) is a declarative framework for building reliable data pipelines on Databricks. Instead of writing imperative code that specifies how to process data step by step, you declare what the final tables should look like, and DLT handles the orchestration, error handling, and data quality enforcement.

1.110.1 Why DLT?

Traditional data pipelines require managing: - Execution order and dependencies - Checkpoint management for streaming - Error handling and retries - Data quality validation - Infrastructure and scaling

DLT abstracts all of this, letting you focus on business logic:

Concern	Traditional Pipeline	DLT Pipeline
Dependency management	Manual task ordering	Automatic from data lineage
Streaming checkpoints	Manual configuration	Automatic
Data quality	Custom validation code	Declarative expectations
Error handling	Try/catch blocks	Built-in retry and recovery
Schema management	Manual DDL	Automatic
Monitoring	Custom logging	Built-in event log

1.110.2 Key Concepts

Pipeline: A collection of DLT table and view definitions that are processed together as a unit.

Dataset: A table or view defined in a DLT pipeline. Datasets can be: - **Streaming tables**—Append-only tables for streaming data - **Materialized views**—Tables that are fully recomputed on each update - **Views**—Intermediate computations not persisted to storage

Expectations: Declarative data quality constraints applied to datasets.

> **Exam Tip:** DLT is heavily tested on the DP-750 exam. Understand the difference between streaming tables (append-only, incremental) and materialized views (full recomputation). Know the three expectation actions (`expect`, `expect_or_drop`, `expect_or_fail`) and when to use each.

1.111 Creating DLT Datasets with Python

1.111.1 Materialized Views

Materialized views are fully recomputed on each pipeline update:

```
import dlt
from pyspark.sql.functions import col, sum, count, avg

@dlt.table(
    comment="Aggregated daily revenue by product category",
    table_properties={"quality": "gold"}
)
def daily_revenue():
    return (
        dlt.read("silver_orders")
        .groupBy("order_date", "product_category")
        .agg(
            sum("total_amount").alias("revenue"),
            count("order_id").alias("order_count"),
            avg("total_amount").alias("avg_order_value")
        )
    )
```

1.111.2 Streaming Tables

Streaming tables process data incrementally and are append-only:

```
import dlt
from pyspark.sql.functions import col, current_timestamp, input_file_name

@dlt.table(
    comment="Raw order events ingested from cloud storage",
    table_properties={"quality": "bronze"}
)
def bronze_orders():
    return (
        spark.readStream
        .format("cloudFiles")
        .option("cloudFiles.format", "json")
        .option("cloudFiles.inferColumnTypes", "true")
        .load("/Volumes/raw/orders/incoming/")
        .withColumn("_ingestion_time", current_timestamp())
        .withColumn("_source_file", input_file_name())
    )
```

1.111.3 Views (Intermediate Computations)

Views are temporary computations that are not persisted:

```
@dlt.view(
    comment="Parsed and validated orders before deduplication"
)
def parsed_orders():
    return (
        dlt.read_stream("bronze_orders")
        .select(
            col("order_id").cast("bigint"),
            col("customer_id").cast("bigint"),
            col("product_name"),
            col("quantity").cast("int"),
            col("unit_price").cast("decimal(10,2)"),
            col("order_date").cast("date"),
            col("status")
        )
    )
```

1.111.4 Reading from Other DLT Datasets

```
# Read from a materialized view or streaming table (batch read)
df = dlt.read("silver_orders")

# Read from a streaming table (streaming read)
df = dlt.read_stream("bronze_orders")
```

> **Exam Tip:** Use `dlt.read()` for batch reads (materialized views) and `dlt.read_stream()` for streaming reads (streaming tables). Using the wrong one will cause errors. If the source is a streaming table and you want incremental processing, always use `dlt.read_stream()`.

1.112 Creating DLT Datasets with SQL

1.112.1 Materialized Views in SQL

```
-- Gold layer: daily revenue summary
CREATE OR REFRESH MATERIALIZED VIEW daily_revenue
COMMENT "Aggregated daily revenue by product category"
AS
SELECT
    order_date,
    product_category,
    SUM(total_amount) AS revenue,
    COUNT(order_id) AS order_count,
    AVG(total_amount) AS avg_order_value
FROM LIVE.silver_orders
GROUP BY order_date, product_category;
```

1.112.2 Streaming Tables in SQL

```
-- Bronze layer: raw order ingestion
CREATE OR REFRESH STREAMING TABLE bronze_orders
COMMENT "Raw order events from cloud storage"
AS SELECT
    *,
    current_timestamp() AS _ingestion_time
FROM cloud_files(
    '/Volumes/raw/orders/incoming/',
    'json',
    map('cloudFiles.inferColumnTypes', 'true')
);
```

1.112.3 Views in SQL

```
-- Intermediate view (not persisted)
CREATE TEMPORARY LIVE VIEW parsed_orders
AS SELECT
    CAST(order_id AS BIGINT) AS order_id,
    CAST(customer_id AS BIGINT) AS customer_id,
    product_name,
    CAST(quantity AS INT) AS quantity,
    CAST(unit_price AS DECIMAL(10,2)) AS unit_price,
    CAST(order_date AS DATE) AS order_date,
    status
FROM LIVE.bronze_orders;
```

1.112.4 Referencing DLT Datasets in SQL

```
-- Reference other DLT datasets using the LIVE schema
SELECT * FROM LIVE.silver_orders;

-- For streaming reads, use the STREAM() function
SELECT * FROM STREAM(LIVE.bronze_orders);
```

Exam Tip: In SQL DLT, use the `LIVE` keyword to reference other datasets in the same pipeline. For streaming reads, wrap the reference in `STREAM()`. In Python DLT, use `dlt.read()` and `dlt.read_stream()`. This is a common source of exam questions.

1.113 Data Quality Expectations

Expectations are DLT's declarative mechanism for enforcing data quality. They define constraints that incoming data must satisfy.

1.113.1 Three Expectation Actions

`@dlt.expect` (Warn): Records that violate the constraint are allowed through, but the violation is logged in metrics:

```
@dlt.expect("valid_order_id", "order_id IS NOT NULL")
@dlt.expect("valid_quantity", "quantity > 0")
@dlt.table
def silver_orders():
    return dlt.read_stream("bronze_orders")
```

`@dlt.expect_or_drop` (Drop): Records that violate the constraint are silently dropped:

```
@dlt.expect_or_drop("valid_order_id", "order_id IS NOT NULL")
@dlt.expect_or_drop("valid_quantity", "quantity > 0")
@dlt.table
def silver_orders():
    return dlt.read_stream("bronze_orders")
```

`@dlt.expect_or_fail` (Fail): The entire pipeline fails if any record violates the constraint:

```
@dlt.expect_or_fail("valid_order_id", "order_id IS NOT NULL")
@dlt.table
def gold_revenue():
    return dlt.read("silver_orders")
```

1.113.2 Multiple Expectations

```
@dlt.expect_all({
    "valid_order_id": "order_id IS NOT NULL",
    "valid_customer": "customer_id IS NOT NULL",
    "valid_quantity": "quantity > 0",
    "valid_price": "unit_price >= 0"
})
@dlt.table
def silver_orders():
    return dlt.read_stream("bronze_orders")

# Drop rows that fail ANY expectation
@dlt.expect_all_or_drop({
    "valid_order_id": "order_id IS NOT NULL",
    "valid_customer": "customer_id IS NOT NULL"
})
@dlt.table
def silver_orders_clean():
    return dlt.read_stream("bronze_orders")
```

```
# Fail if ANY expectation is violated
@dlt.expect_all_or_fail({
    "valid_totals": "total_amount > 0",
    "valid_date": "order_date <= current_date()"
})
@dlt.table
def gold_validated():
    return dlt.read("silver_orders")
```

1.113.3 SQL Expectations

```
-- EXPECT (warn only)
CREATE OR REFRESH STREAMING TABLE silver_orders (
    CONSTRAINT valid_order_id EXPECT (order_id IS NOT NULL),
    CONSTRAINT valid_quantity EXPECT (quantity > 0),
    CONSTRAINT valid_price EXPECT (unit_price >= 0)
)
AS SELECT * FROM STREAM(LIVE.bronze_orders);

-- EXPECT with ON VIOLATION DROP ROW
CREATE OR REFRESH STREAMING TABLE silver_orders_clean (
    CONSTRAINT valid_order_id EXPECT (order_id IS NOT NULL) ON VIOLATION DROP ROW,
    CONSTRAINT valid_customer EXPECT (customer_id IS NOT NULL) ON VIOLATION DROP ROW
)
AS SELECT * FROM STREAM(LIVE.bronze_orders);

-- EXPECT with ON VIOLATION FAIL UPDATE
CREATE OR REFRESH STREAMING TABLE gold_validated (
    CONSTRAINT valid_totals EXPECT (total_amount > 0) ON VIOLATION FAIL UPDATE
)
AS SELECT * FROM STREAM(LIVE.silver_orders);
```

Action	Python	SQL	Behavior
Warn	`@dlt.expect`	`EXPECT (...)`	Log violation, keep record
Drop	`@dlt.expect_or_drop`	`EXPECT (...) ON VIOLATION DROP ROW`	Silently drop record
Fail	`@dlt.expect_or_fail`	`EXPECT (...) ON VIOLATION FAIL UPDATE`	Fail entire pipeline

> **Exam Tip:** This is one of the most heavily tested DLT topics. You must know all three expectation actions and their behaviors. A common exam pattern presents a scenario and asks which expectation action ensures bad data never enters the table (answer: `expect_or_drop` or `expect_or_fail`, depending on whether the pipeline should continue or stop).

1.114 Complete Medallion Pipeline Example

1.114.1 Python Pipeline

```
import dlt
from pyspark.sql.functions import *
```

```
# ---- BRONZE LAYER ----

@dlt.table(
    comment="Raw order events from cloud storage",
    table_properties={"quality": "bronze"}
)
def bronze_orders():
    return (
        spark.readStream
        .format("cloudFiles")
        .option("cloudFiles.format", "json")
        .option("cloudFiles.inferColumnTypes", "true")
        .load("/Volumes/raw/orders/incoming/")
        .withColumn("_ingestion_time", current_timestamp())
        .withColumn("_source_file", input_file_name())
    )

# ---- SILVER LAYER ----

@dlt.expect_or_drop("valid_order_id", "order_id IS NOT NULL")
@dlt.expect_or_drop("valid_customer", "customer_id IS NOT NULL")
@dlt.expect("valid_quantity", "quantity > 0")
@dlt.expect("valid_price", "unit_price >= 0")
@dlt.table(
    comment="Cleansed and validated orders",
    table_properties={"quality": "silver"}
)
def silver_orders():
    return (
        dlt.read_stream("bronze_orders")
        .select(
            col("order_id").cast("bigint").alias("order_id"),
            col("customer_id").cast("bigint").alias("customer_id"),
            trim(col("product_name")).alias("product_name"),
            col("quantity").cast("int").alias("quantity"),
            col("unit_price").cast("decimal(10,2)").alias("unit_price"),
            (col("quantity") * col("unit_price")).alias("total_amount"),
            col("order_date").cast("date").alias("order_date"),
            upper(trim(col("status"))).alias("status"),
            col("_ingestion_time")
        )
    )

# ---- GOLD LAYER ----

@dlt.table(
    comment="Daily revenue aggregation by product",
    table_properties={"quality": "gold"}
)
def gold_daily_revenue():
    return (
        dlt.read("silver_orders")
        .filter(col("status") == "COMPLETED")
        .groupBy("order_date", "product_name")
        .agg(
            count("order_id").alias("order_count"),
            sum("total_amount").alias("revenue"),
            avg("total_amount").alias("avg_order_value")
        )
```

```
    )

@dlt.table(
    comment="Customer lifetime value summary",
    table_properties={"quality": "gold"}
)
def gold_customer_ltv():
    return (
        dlt.read("silver_orders")
        .groupBy("customer_id")
        .agg(
            count("order_id").alias("total_orders"),
            sum("total_amount").alias("lifetime_value"),
            min("order_date").alias("first_order"),
            max("order_date").alias("last_order"),
            avg("total_amount").alias("avg_order_value")
        )
    )
```

1.114.2 SQL Pipeline

```
-- BRONZE LAYER
CREATE OR REFRESH STREAMING TABLE bronze_orders
COMMENT "Raw order events from cloud storage"
TBLPROPERTIES ("quality" = "bronze")
AS SELECT
    *,
    current_timestamp() AS _ingestion_time,
    input_file_name() AS _source_file
FROM cloud_files(
    '/Volumes/raw/orders/incoming/',
    'json',
    map('cloudFiles.inferColumnTypes', 'true')
);

-- SILVER LAYER
CREATE OR REFRESH STREAMING TABLE silver_orders (
    CONSTRAINT valid_order_id EXPECT (order_id IS NOT NULL) ON VIOLATION DROP ROW,
    CONSTRAINT valid_customer EXPECT (customer_id IS NOT NULL) ON VIOLATION DROP ROW,
    CONSTRAINT valid_quantity EXPECT (quantity > 0),
    CONSTRAINT valid_price EXPECT (unit_price >= 0)
)
COMMENT "Cleansed and validated orders"
TBLPROPERTIES ("quality" = "silver")
AS SELECT
    CAST(order_id AS BIGINT) AS order_id,
    CAST(customer_id AS BIGINT) AS customer_id,
    TRIM(product_name) AS product_name,
    CAST(quantity AS INT) AS quantity,
    CAST(unit_price AS DECIMAL(10,2)) AS unit_price,
    quantity * unit_price AS total_amount,
    CAST(order_date AS DATE) AS order_date,
    UPPER(TRIM(status)) AS status,
    _ingestion_time
FROM STREAM(LIVE.bronze_orders);

-- GOLD LAYER
CREATE OR REFRESH MATERIALIZED VIEW gold_daily_revenue
```

```
COMMENT "Daily revenue aggregation by product"
TBLPROPERTIES ("quality" = "gold")
AS SELECT
    order_date,
    product_name,
    COUNT(order_id) AS order_count,
    SUM(total_amount) AS revenue,
    AVG(total_amount) AS avg_order_value
FROM LIVE.silver_orders
WHERE status = 'COMPLETED'
GROUP BY order_date, product_name;
```

1.115 Pipeline Configuration

1.115.1 Pipeline Settings

DLT pipelines are configured through the Databricks UI or API:

```
{
    "name": "orders-medallion-pipeline",
    "target": "analytics",
    "catalog": "prod",
    "libraries": [
        {"notebook": {"path": "/Repos/data-engineering/pipelines/orders_pipeline"}}
    ],
    "configuration": {
        "source_path": "/Volumes/raw/orders/incoming/"
    },
    "clusters": [
        {
            "label": "default",
            "autoscale": {
                "min_workers": 1,
                "max_workers": 4,
                "mode": "ENHANCED"
            }
        }
    ],
    "channel": "CURRENT",
    "photon": true,
    "development": false,
    "continuous": false
}
```

1.115.2 Development vs. Production Mode

Feature	Development Mode	Production Mode
Cluster reuse	Clusters are reused across updates	New clusters for each update
Error handling	Errors are surfaced immediately	Automatic retries on failures
Data reprocessing	Can reset and reprocess all data	Incremental processing only
Cost	Lower (reused clusters)	Higher (fresh clusters)

Exam Tip: Development mode is for iterative pipeline development; production mode is for reliable scheduled execution. Know that development mode reuses clusters (faster iterations) while production mode creates fresh clusters (clean state, more reliable).

1.115.3 Continuous vs. Triggered Execution

Triggered: The pipeline runs once to process all available data, then stops. Ideal for scheduled execution.
Continuous: The pipeline runs continuously, processing new data as it arrives. Lower latency but higher compute cost.

1.115.4 Pipeline Parameters

Access pipeline configuration parameters in your code:

```
# Access pipeline configuration
source_path = spark.conf.get("source_path")

@dlt.table
def bronze_data():
    return (
        spark.readStream
        .format("cloudFiles")
        .option("cloudFiles.format", "json")
        .load(source_path)
    )
```

1.116 The DLT Event Log

The event log provides detailed information about pipeline execution:

```
-- Query the event log for a pipeline
SELECT
    timestamp,
    level,
    message,
    details
FROM event_log(TABLE(analytics.silver_orders))
ORDER BY timestamp DESC;

-- Query data quality metrics
SELECT
    timestamp,
    details:flow_name AS dataset,
    details:expectations AS expectations
FROM event_log(TABLE(analytics.silver_orders))
WHERE event_type = 'flow_progress'
  AND details:expectations IS NOT NULL;
```

The event log captures: - Pipeline start/stop events - Dataset creation and update events - Data quality expectation results (pass/fail counts) - Error messages and stack traces - Cluster lifecycle events

Exam Tip: The event log is the primary tool for monitoring and troubleshooting DLT pipelines. Know that expectation metrics (number of records that passed/failed each constraint) are available in the event log. This is how you track data quality over time.

1.117 Advanced DLT Patterns

1.117.1 Apply Changes (CDC/SCD)

DLT provides a built-in mechanism for processing change data capture (CDC) feeds:

```
import dlt
from pyspark.sql.functions import col

# Define the source CDC stream
@dlt.view
def customers_cdc():
    return dlt.read_stream("bronze_customer_changes")

# Apply changes to maintain a Type 1 SCD table
dlt.create_streaming_table("silver_customers")

dlt.apply_changes(
    target="silver_customers",
    source="customers_cdc",
    keys=["customer_id"],
    sequence_by=col("event_timestamp"),
    apply_as_deletes=expr("operation = 'DELETE'"),
    apply_as_truncates=expr("operation = 'TRUNCATE'"),
    column_list=[
        "customer_id", "name", "email", "phone", "address"
    ]
)

# SCD Type 2 with apply_changes
dlt.create_streaming_table("silver_customers_scd2")

dlt.apply_changes(
    target="silver_customers_scd2",
    source="customers_cdc",
    keys=["customer_id"],
    sequence_by=col("event_timestamp"),
    stored_as_scd_type=2  # Enable SCD Type 2
)
```

1.117.2 Parameterized Expectations

```
# Dynamic quality thresholds from configuration
min_quantity = int(spark.conf.get("min_valid_quantity", "0"))

@dlt.expect("valid_quantity", f"quantity > {min_quantity}")
@dlt.table
def silver_orders():
    return dlt.read_stream("bronze_orders")
```

1.118 Chapter Summary

In this chapter, you learned:

- **DLT** is a declarative framework that automates dependency management, checkpointing, and error handling

- **Streaming tables** process data incrementally (append-only); **materialized views** recompute fully on each update
- **Expectations** enforce data quality: `expect` (warn), `expect_or_drop` (drop), `expect_or_fail` (fail)
- In Python, use `dlt.read()` and `dlt.read_stream()`; in SQL, use `LIVE.` and `STREAM(LIVE.)`
- **Development mode** reuses clusters for fast iteration; **production mode** creates fresh clusters for reliability
- The **event log** provides pipeline monitoring, data quality metrics, and troubleshooting information
- **`apply_changes`** handles CDC/SCD patterns, including Type 1 and Type 2 slowly changing dimensions

---

1.119 Practice Questions

Question 1: What is the difference between a streaming table and a materialized view in DLT?
A. Streaming tables store data; materialized views do not B. Streaming tables process data incrementally; materialized views recompute fully C. Materialized views support expectations; streaming tables do not D. Streaming tables can only read from Kafka sources

Question 2: Which expectation action silently removes records that violate a data quality constraint?
A. `@dlt.expect` B. `@dlt.expect_or_drop` C. `@dlt.expect_or_fail` D. `@dlt.expect_or_quarantine`

Question 3: In a SQL DLT pipeline, how do you reference another dataset defined in the same pipeline?
A. Use the dataset name directly B. Use the `LIVE.` prefix C. Use the `DLT.` prefix D. Use the `PIPELINE.` prefix

Question 4: A DLT pipeline has expectations that log violations but allow records through. The data engineering team wants to track how many records fail each expectation over time. Where can they find this information?
A. The Delta Lake transaction log B. The DLT event log C. The Unity Catalog audit log D. The Spark driver logs

Question 5: Which DLT function is used for processing CDC feeds and maintaining SCD tables?
A. `dlt.merge()` B. `dlt.apply_changes()` C. `dlt.upsert()` D. `dlt.cdc_process()`

Question 6: In Python DLT, which function reads from a streaming table incrementally?
A. `dlt.read()` B. `dlt.read_stream()` C. `dlt.stream()` D. `spark.readStream.table()`

Question 7: What happens when a record violates an `@dlt.expect_or_fail` constraint?
A. The record is dropped silently B. The record is written to a quarantine table C. The entire pipeline update fails D. The violation is logged but the record is kept

Question 8: Which SQL syntax creates a streaming table with data quality constraints that drop violating rows?
A. `CREATE STREAMING TABLE t (CONSTRAINT c EXPECT (col > 0)) AS ...` B. `CREATE STREAMING TABLE t (CONSTRAINT c EXPECT (col > 0) ON VIOLATION DROP ROW) AS ...` C. `CREATE STREAMING TABLE t (CONSTRAINT c CHECK (col > 0) DROP ) AS ...` D. `CREATE STREAMING TABLE t WHERE col > 0 AS ...`

Question 9: In DLT development mode, what happens to clusters between pipeline updates?
A. Clusters are terminated and recreated B. Clusters are reused for faster iteration C. Clusters are scaled down to minimum size D. Clusters are paused and resumed

Question 10: A data engineer wants to create a DLT dataset that computes intermediate results but does not persist them to storage. Which dataset type should they use?
A. Streaming table B. Materialized view C. View D. Temporary table

---

1.120 Answer Explanations

Question 1: B. Streaming tables process data incrementally (append-only), while materialized views fully recompute their results on each pipeline update. Both persist data to storage. Reference: DLT dataset types documentation.

Question 2: B. `@dlt.expect_or_drop` silently removes records that violate the constraint. `@dlt.expect` logs violations but keeps records. `@dlt.expect_or_fail` stops the pipeline. There is no `expect_or_quarantine` action. Reference: DLT expectations documentation.

Question 3: B. In SQL DLT, use the `LIVE.` prefix to reference other datasets in the same pipeline (e.g., `SELECT * FROM LIVE.silver_orders`). For streaming reads, use `STREAM(LIVE.dataset_name)`. Reference: DLT SQL reference documentation.

Question 4: B. The DLT event log captures expectation metrics, including the number of records that passed and failed each constraint. This is the primary monitoring mechanism for data quality in DLT pipelines. Reference: DLT event log documentation.

Question 5: B. `dlt.apply_changes()` processes CDC feeds and can maintain both SCD Type 1 and SCD Type 2 tables. It handles inserts, updates, and deletes based on a sequence column. Reference: DLT apply_changes documentation.

Question 6: B. `dlt.read_stream()` performs a streaming (incremental) read from a DLT dataset. `dlt.read()` performs a batch read. Using `spark.readStream.table()` directly is not the recommended pattern within DLT. Reference: DLT Python API documentation.

Question 7: C. `@dlt.expect_or_fail` causes the entire pipeline update to fail if any record violates the constraint. This is the strictest enforcement action, used when data quality violations must never be tolerated. Reference: DLT expectations documentation.

Question 8: B. The SQL syntax `CONSTRAINT c EXPECT (col > 0) ON VIOLATION DROP ROW` creates an expectation that drops violating rows. Without `ON VIOLATION DROP ROW`, the default behavior is to log the violation but keep the record. Reference: DLT SQL expectations syntax.

Question 9: B. In development mode, DLT reuses clusters between pipeline updates, enabling faster iteration during development. In production mode, fresh clusters are created for each update for maximum reliability. Reference: DLT pipeline modes documentation.

Question 10: C. A DLT view computes intermediate results without persisting them to storage. Views are useful for breaking complex transformations into readable steps without incurring the cost of materializing each intermediate result. Reference: DLT dataset types documentation. # Chapter 11: Workflow Orchestration and Job Scheduling

Meridian Certification Press—Microsoft DP-750: Implementing Azure Databricks Study Guide 2026

1.121 Learning Objectives

After completing this chapter, you will be able to:

- Create and configure Databricks Workflows with multiple tasks
- Implement task dependencies and execution flow
- Configure job schedules using cron expressions and triggers
- Parameterize jobs with task values and job parameters
- Implement error handling with retries and conditional tasks
- Manage job clusters and compute resources
- Integrate Databricks Workflows with external orchestrators

1.122 Introduction to Databricks Workflows

Databricks Workflows is the native orchestration service for running data pipelines, ML workloads, and analytics jobs on Azure Databricks. A workflow (job) consists of one or more tasks that can run sequentially, in parallel, or in complex dependency graphs.

1.122.1 Key Components

Job: A named unit of work containing one or more tasks, a schedule, and configuration settings.

Task: A single unit of execution within a job. Task types include: - **Notebook task**—Runs a Databricks notebook - **Python script task**—Runs a Python file - **JAR task** – Runs a Java/Scala JAR - **SQL task**—Runs SQL queries or a SQL dashboard - **DLT pipeline task**—Triggers a Delta Live Tables pipeline - **dbt task**—Runs a dbt project - **Run Job task**—Triggers another Databricks job - **If/Else condition task**—Conditional execution - **For Each task**—Iterates over a collection

Run: A single execution of a job, containing the results and metadata for that execution.

1.122.2 Task Dependencies

Tasks within a job can be organized into a directed acyclic graph (DAG):

```
        ┌─── Task B ───┐
        |              |
Task A ─┤              ├─ Task D ─ Task E
        |              |
        └─── Task C ───┘
```

In this example: - Task A runs first - Tasks B and C run in parallel after A completes - Task D runs after both B and C complete - Task E runs after D completes

> **Exam Tip:** Databricks Workflows support parallel execution of independent tasks within a job. Tasks run in parallel by default unless an explicit dependency is defined. The exam tests your ability to design task dependency graphs for given scenarios.

1.123 Creating Jobs

1.123.1 Using the UI

1. Navigate to **Workflows** in the left sidebar
2. Click **Create Job**
3. Add tasks and configure dependencies
4. Set the schedule and cluster configuration
5. Save and optionally run immediately

1.123.2 Using the Databricks CLI

```
# Create a job from a JSON configuration
databricks jobs create --json '{
    "name": "daily-etl-pipeline",
    "tasks": [
        {
            "task_key": "ingest_data",
            "notebook_task": {
                "notebook_path": "/Repos/data-engineering/pipelines/01_ingest"
            },
            "job_cluster_key": "etl_cluster"
        },
        {
            "task_key": "transform_data",
            "depends_on": [{"task_key": "ingest_data"}],
            "notebook_task": {
                "notebook_path": "/Repos/data-engineering/pipelines/02_transform"
            },
            "job_cluster_key": "etl_cluster"
        },
        {
            "task_key": "validate_data",
            "depends_on": [{"task_key": "transform_data"}],
```

```
            "notebook_task": {
                "notebook_path": "/Repos/data-engineering/pipelines/03_validate"
            },
            "job_cluster_key": "etl_cluster"
        }
    ],
    "job_clusters": [
        {
            "job_cluster_key": "etl_cluster",
            "new_cluster": {
                "spark_version": "14.3.x-scala2.12",
                "node_type_id": "Standard_D4ds_v5",
                "num_workers": 4,
                "data_security_mode": "SINGLE_USER"
            }
        }
    ],
    "schedule": {
        "quartz_cron_expression": "0 0 6 * * ?",
        "timezone_id": "America/New_York"
    }
}'
```

1.123.3 Using the REST API

```python
import requests
import json

# Create a job via the REST API
url = f"https://{workspace_url}/api/2.1/jobs/create"
headers = {"Authorization": f"Bearer {token}"}

job_config = {
    "name": "daily-etl-pipeline",
    "tasks": [
        {
            "task_key": "ingest",
            "notebook_task": {
                "notebook_path": "/Repos/data-engineering/pipelines/01_ingest",
                "base_parameters": {
                    "start_date": "2026-01-01",
                    "environment": "production"
                }
            },
            "job_cluster_key": "etl_cluster"
        }
    ],
    "job_clusters": [
        {
            "job_cluster_key": "etl_cluster",
            "new_cluster": {
                "spark_version": "14.3.x-scala2.12",
                "node_type_id": "Standard_D4ds_v5",
                "num_workers": 2
            }
        }
    ]
}
```

```
response = requests.post(url, headers=headers, json=job_config)
job_id = response.json()["job_id"]
```

1.124 Task Types in Detail

1.124.1 Notebook Tasks

The most common task type. Runs a notebook and can pass/receive parameters:

```
{
    "task_key": "process_orders",
    "notebook_task": {
        "notebook_path": "/Repos/data-engineering/pipelines/process_orders",
        "base_parameters": {
            "date": "{{job.start_time.iso_date}}",
            "mode": "production"
        },
        "source": "GIT"
    }
}
```

1.124.2 SQL Tasks

Execute SQL queries, files, or alert conditions:

```
{
    "task_key": "update_summary",
    "sql_task": {
        "query": {
            "query_id": "abc123-query-id"
        },
        "warehouse_id": "warehouse-id-123"
    }
}
```

1.124.3 DLT Pipeline Tasks

Trigger a Delta Live Tables pipeline:

```
{
    "task_key": "run_dlt_pipeline",
    "pipeline_task": {
        "pipeline_id": "pipeline-id-123",
        "full_refresh": false
    }
}
```

1.124.4 Python Script Tasks

Run a Python file from a workspace path or Git repository:

```
{
    "task_key": "run_script",
```

```
    "python_wheel_task": {
        "package_name": "my_etl_package",
        "entry_point": "main",
        "parameters": ["--date", "2026-03-01"]
    }
}
```

1.124.5 If/Else Condition Tasks

Conditionally execute downstream tasks based on a condition:

```
{
    "task_key": "check_data_quality",
    "condition_task": {
        "op": "GREATER_THAN",
        "left": "{{tasks.validate.values.error_count}}",
        "right": "0"
    }
}
```

1.124.6 For Each Tasks

Iterate over a collection and execute a nested task for each element:

```
{
    "task_key": "process_regions",
    "for_each_task": {
        "inputs": "[\"us-east\", \"us-west\", \"eu-west\", \"ap-south\"]",
        "task": {
            "task_key": "process_region",
            "notebook_task": {
                "notebook_path": "/pipelines/process_region",
                "base_parameters": {
                    "region": "{{input}}"
                }
            }
        }
    }
}
```

> **Exam Tip:** Know all the major task types, especially notebook, SQL, DLT pipeline, if/else condition, and for-each. The exam commonly tests scenarios where you must choose the appropriate task type or design a multi-task workflow with conditions and iterations.

1.125 Job Scheduling

1.125.1 Cron-Based Scheduling

Databricks uses Quartz cron expressions for scheduling:

```
┌─────────
second (0-59)│
┌───────── minute (0-59)│
│ ┌───────── hour (0-23)│
│ │ ┌───────── day of month (1-31)│
```

```
│ │ │ ┌────── month (1-12)│
│ │ │ │ ┌────── day of week (1-7, 1=Sunday)│
│ │ │ │ │
* * * * * *
```

Common schedule examples:

```
0 0 6 * * ?          Every day at 6:00 AM
0 0 */2 * * ?        Every 2 hours
0 30 8 ? * MON-FRI   Weekdays at 8:30 AM
0 0 0 1 * ?          First day of every month at midnight
0 0 6,18 * * ?       Twice daily at 6 AM and 6 PM
0 */15 * * * ?       Every 15 minutes
```

1.125.2 File Arrival Triggers

Jobs can be triggered when new files arrive in a cloud storage location:

```
{
    "trigger": {
        "file_arrival": {
            "url": "abfss://container@storageaccount.dfs.core.windows.net/incoming/",
            "min_time_between_triggers_seconds": 60,
            "wait_after_last_change_seconds": 30
        }
    }
}
```

1.125.3 Continuous Jobs

For low-latency requirements, jobs can run continuously:

```
{
    "trigger": {
        "periodic": {
            "interval": 60,
            "unit": "SECONDS"
        }
    },
    "max_concurrent_runs": 1
}
```

> **Exam Tip:** Know the three trigger types: **cron schedule** (time-based), **file arrival** (event-based), and **continuous/periodic** (always running). File arrival triggers are useful for event-driven architectures. The `max_concurrent_runs` setting prevents overlapping executions.

1.126 Job Parameters and Task Values

1.126.1 Job Parameters

Pass parameters to a job at run time:

```
# In the notebook, access job parameters
date_param = dbutils.widgets.get("date")
environment = dbutils.widgets.get("environment")
```

1.126.2 Task Values (Passing Data Between Tasks)

Tasks can share values with downstream tasks using `dbutils.jobs.taskValues`:

```
# Task A: Set a task value
row_count = df.count()
dbutils.jobs.taskValues.set(key="row_count", value=row_count)
dbutils.jobs.taskValues.set(key="status", value="success")

# Task B: Read a task value from Task A
row_count = dbutils.jobs.taskValues.get(
    taskKey="task_a",
    key="row_count",
    default=0
)
status = dbutils.jobs.taskValues.get(
    taskKey="task_a",
    key="status",
    default="unknown"
)

print(f"Task A processed {row_count} rows with status: {status}")
```

1.126.3 Dynamic Parameters

Use job-level dynamic variables in task parameters:

```
{
    "base_parameters": {
        "run_date": "{{job.start_time.iso_date}}",
        "run_id": "{{job.run_id}}",
        "task_name": "{{task.task_key}}"
    }
}
```

Available dynamic variables: - `{{job.run_id}}`—Unique run identifier - `{{job.start_time.iso_date}}`—Job start date (YYYY-MM-DD) - `{{job.start_time.iso_datetime}}`—Full ISO timestamp - `{{task.task_key}}` – Current task key name

> **Exam Tip:** `dbutils.jobs.taskValues` is the mechanism for passing data between tasks. Know the `set()` and `get()` methods, and that the `get()` method requires the `taskKey` parameter to specify which upstream task to read from. This is a commonly tested topic.

1.127 Error Handling and Retries

1.127.1 Task-Level Retries

```
{
    "task_key": "flaky_api_call",
    "max_retries": 3,
    "min_retry_interval_millis": 30000,
    "retry_on_timeout": true,
    "notebook_task": {
        "notebook_path": "/pipelines/call_external_api"
    }
}
```

1.127.2 Timeout Configuration

```
{
    "task_key": "long_running_task",
    "timeout_seconds": 3600,
    "notebook_task": {
        "notebook_path": "/pipelines/heavy_transformation"
    }
}
```

1.127.3 Conditional Failure Handling

Use if/else tasks to handle failures gracefully:

```
Task A (main work)├──
 On Success → Task B (next step)└──
 On Failure → Task C (error notification)
                   └── Task D (cleanup)
```

```
{
    "task_key": "notify_failure",
    "depends_on": [
        {
            "task_key": "main_processing",
            "outcome": "failed"
        }
    ],
    "notebook_task": {
        "notebook_path": "/pipelines/send_alert"
    }
}
```

1.127.4 Email Notifications

```
{
    "email_notifications": {
        "on_start": ["team@company.com"],
        "on_success": ["team@company.com"],
        "on_failure": ["team@company.com", "oncall@company.com"],
        "on_duration_warning_threshold_exceeded": ["team@company.com"]
    },
    "notification_settings": {
        "no_alert_for_skipped_runs": true,
        "no_alert_for_canceled_runs": true
    }
}
```

1.128 Compute Configuration

1.128.1 Job Clusters

Job clusters are created for the duration of a job run and terminated when the job completes:

```
{
    "job_clusters": [
        {
            "job_cluster_key": "etl_cluster",
            "new_cluster": {
                "spark_version": "14.3.x-scala2.12",
                "node_type_id": "Standard_D4ds_v5",
                "num_workers": 4,
                "data_security_mode": "SINGLE_USER",
                "azure_attributes": {
                    "first_on_demand": 1,
                    "availability": "SPOT_WITH_FALLBACK_AZURE"
                }
            }
        }
    ]
}
```

1.128.2 Shared Job Clusters

Multiple tasks can share the same job cluster to reduce startup overhead:

```
{
    "tasks": [
        {
            "task_key": "task_1",
            "job_cluster_key": "shared_etl_cluster",
            "notebook_task": { "notebook_path": "/pipelines/step1" }
        },
        {
            "task_key": "task_2",
            "depends_on": [{"task_key": "task_1"}],
            "job_cluster_key": "shared_etl_cluster",
            "notebook_task": { "notebook_path": "/pipelines/step2" }
        }
    ]
}
```

1.128.3 Existing Clusters

Tasks can run on an existing all-purpose cluster (useful for development):

```
{
    "task_key": "dev_task",
    "existing_cluster_id": "0123-456789-abcdef"
}
```

1.128.4 Serverless Compute

```
{
    "task_key": "serverless_task",
    "notebook_task": { "notebook_path": "/pipelines/transform" },
    "environment_key": "default"
}
```

Exam Tip: For production jobs, use **job clusters** (lower cost, ephemeral). Multiple tasks can share a job cluster to reduce startup time. Using an **existing all-purpose cluster** is only recommended for development. **Serverless compute** eliminates cluster management entirely.

1.129 CI/CD Integration

1.129.1 Databricks Asset Bundles (DABs)

```
# databricks.yml
bundle:
  name: etl-pipeline

resources:
  jobs:
    daily_etl:
      name: daily-etl-pipeline
      tasks:
        - task_key: ingest
          notebook_task:
            notebook_path: ./notebooks/01_ingest.py
          job_cluster_key: etl_cluster
        - task_key: transform
          depends_on:
            - task_key: ingest
          notebook_task:
            notebook_path: ./notebooks/02_transform.py
          job_cluster_key: etl_cluster
      job_clusters:
        - job_cluster_key: etl_cluster
          new_cluster:
            spark_version: 14.3.x-scala2.12
            node_type_id: Standard_D4ds_v5
            num_workers: 4

targets:
  dev:
    default: true
    workspace:
      host: https://adb-1234567890.azuredatabricks.net
  prod:
    workspace:
      host: https://adb-0987654321.azuredatabricks.net
```

```
# Deploy with Databricks Asset Bundles
databricks bundle validate
databricks bundle deploy --target prod
databricks bundle run daily_etl --target prod
```

1.130 Chapter Summary

In this chapter, you learned:

- Databricks Workflows orchestrate multi-task jobs with **DAG-based dependencies**

- Task types include **notebook, SQL, DLT pipeline, Python script, if/else, and for-each**
- Jobs can be triggered by **cron schedules, file arrival events**, or run **continuously**
- **Task values** (`dbutils.jobs.taskValues`) pass data between tasks within a job
- **Error handling** includes retries, timeouts, conditional failure paths, and email notifications
- **Job clusters** are preferred for production; multiple tasks can **share** a job cluster
- **Databricks Asset Bundles** enable CI/CD with environment-specific deployments

---

1.131 Practice Questions

Question 1: A data engineer needs to pass the row count from an ingestion task to a validation task. Which mechanism should they use?

A. Notebook widgets B. `dbutils.jobs.taskValues` C. Spark configuration variables D. Temporary Delta tables

Question 2: Which task type allows iterating over a list of regions and running a notebook for each region in parallel?

A. If/Else condition task B. SQL task C. For Each task D. Run Job task

Question 3: A job should only run when new files arrive in an ADLS Gen2 container. Which trigger type should be configured?

A. Cron schedule B. File arrival trigger C. Continuous trigger D. Webhook trigger

Question 4: Which cluster type provides the lowest cost for production job execution?

A. All-purpose cluster B. Job cluster C. SQL warehouse D. Interactive cluster

Question 5: A task fails intermittently due to a flaky external API. How should the data engineer handle this?

A. Set `max_retries` on the task with a retry interval B. Wrap the API call in an infinite loop C. Use an all-purpose cluster for better stability D. Disable the task and process manually

Question 6: In a job with tasks A, B, C, and D where B and C both depend on A, and D depends on both B and C, what is the execution order?

A. A, B, C, D (all sequential) B. A, then B and C in parallel, then D C. A and B in parallel, then C, then D D. All four tasks run in parallel

Question 7: Which cron expression schedules a job to run every day at 6:00 AM?

A. `0 6 * * *` B. `0 0 6 * * ?` C. `6 0 * * * ?` D. `0 * 6 * * ?`

Question 8: What is the purpose of `max_concurrent_runs` in a job configuration?

A. Limits the number of parallel tasks within a job B. Limits the number of workers in the job cluster C. Prevents multiple instances of the same job from running simultaneously D. Sets the maximum number of retries for a failed run

---

1.132 Answer Explanations

Question 1: B. `dbutils.jobs.taskValues.set()` and `get()` are the designated mechanism for passing values between tasks within a Databricks job. The ingestion task sets a value, and the validation task reads it using the task key. Reference: Databricks task values documentation.

Question 2: C. The For Each task iterates over a collection (like a list of regions) and runs a nested task for each element. Elements can be processed in parallel. Reference: Databricks for-each task documentation.

Question 3: B. File arrival triggers start a job when new files are detected in a specified cloud storage location. This is ideal for event-driven pipelines. Reference: Databricks file arrival trigger documentation.

Question 4: B. Job clusters are created for the duration of a job and terminated when complete. They have a lower DBU rate than all-purpose clusters and are the recommended choice for production workloads. Reference: Databricks cluster types and pricing.

Question 5: A. Setting `max_retries` with a `min_retry_interval_millis` is the standard approach for handling intermittent failures. The task will automatically retry the specified number of times before marking as failed. Reference: Databricks task retry configuration.

Question 6: B. A runs first (no dependencies). B and C both depend only on A, so they run in parallel once A completes. D depends on both B and C, so it runs only after both complete. This is a standard DAG execution pattern. Reference: Databricks task dependency documentation.

Question 7: B. Quartz cron expressions have six fields (second, minute, hour, day-of-month, month, day-of-week). `0 0 6 * * ?` means second 0, minute 0, hour 6, every day, every month, any day of week. Reference: Quartz cron expression format.

Question 8: C. `max_concurrent_runs` limits how many instances of the same job can run at the same time. Setting it to 1 prevents overlapping executions, which is important for jobs that should not run concurrently. Reference: Databricks job configuration documentation. # Chapter 12: Pipeline Monitoring, Alerting, and Troubleshooting

Meridian Certification Press—Microsoft DP-750: Implementing Azure Databricks Study Guide 2026

1.133 Learning Objectives

After completing this chapter, you will be able to:

- Monitor pipeline health using the Databricks UI, system tables, and APIs
- Configure alerts for job failures, SLA violations, and data quality issues
- Interpret Spark UI metrics to diagnose performance problems
- Troubleshoot common pipeline failures including OOM errors, data skew, and shuffle issues
- Use the DLT event log for pipeline diagnostics
- Implement observability best practices for production pipelines

---

1.134 Monitoring Overview

Effective pipeline monitoring requires visibility into three areas:

1. **Execution monitoring**—Did the pipeline run? Did it succeed or fail?
2. **Performance monitoring**—How long did it take? Is it within SLA?
3. **Data quality monitoring**—Is the output data correct and complete?

Azure Databricks provides multiple tools for monitoring:

Tool	Purpose	Access
Workflows UI	Job run history, task status, duration	Workspace sidebar
Spark UI	Stage-level execution metrics, DAG visualization	Cluster details
System tables	Queryable audit, billing, and usage data	`system.` catalog
DLT Event Log	Pipeline events and data quality metrics	SQL query
REST API	Programmatic access to run results	HTTP endpoints
Azure Monitor	Platform-level diagnostics and log analytics	Azure Portal

---

1.135 Job Monitoring

1.135.1 Workflows UI

The Workflows UI provides a visual dashboard for all job runs:

- **Run history**—View all past runs with status (succeeded, failed, timed out, cancelled)
- **Task-level details**—Drill into individual tasks to see logs, duration, and output

- **Gantt chart**—Visualize parallel task execution and timing
- **Error messages**—View stack traces for failed tasks

1.135.2 Run Status via API

```
import requests

# Get job run details
url = f"https://{workspace_url}/api/2.1/jobs/runs/get"
headers = {"Authorization": f"Bearer {token}"}
params = {"run_id": run_id}

response = requests.get(url, headers=headers, params=params)
run_info = response.json()

print(f"Status: {run_info['state']['result_state']}")
print(f"Duration: {run_info['run_duration'] / 1000:.0f} seconds")
for task in run_info['tasks']:
    print(f"  Task: {task['task_key']}, Status: {task['state']['result_state']}")
```

1.135.3 Run Statuses

State	Result State	Meaning
TERMINATED	SUCCESS	Job completed successfully
TERMINATED	FAILED	One or more tasks failed
TERMINATED	TIMED_OUT	Job exceeded its timeout
TERMINATED	CANCELED	Job was manually cancelled
RUNNING	—	Job is currently executing
PENDING	—	Job is waiting for resources
SKIPPED	—	Task was skipped (conditional)

1.136 System Tables

Databricks system tables provide queryable access to operational data across the workspace:

1.136.1 Audit Logs

```
-- Query audit logs for data access events
SELECT
    event_time,
    action_name,
    user_identity.email AS user_email,
    request_params.full_name_arg AS table_name,
    source_ip_address
FROM system.access.audit
WHERE action_name IN ('getTable', 'createTable', 'deleteTable')
  AND event_time > current_timestamp() - INTERVAL 7 DAYS
ORDER BY event_time DESC;
```

1.136.2 Billing and Usage

```sql
-- Query compute usage and costs
SELECT
    usage_date,
    workspace_id,
    sku_name,
    usage_quantity AS dbu_count,
    usage_metadata.cluster_id,
    usage_metadata.job_id
FROM system.billing.usage
WHERE usage_date >= current_date() - INTERVAL 30 DAYS
  AND sku_name LIKE '%JOBS%'
ORDER BY usage_date DESC;
```

1.136.3 Table Lineage

```sql
-- Query table-level lineage
SELECT
    source_table_full_name,
    target_table_full_name,
    source_type,
    target_type,
    event_time
FROM system.access.table_lineage
WHERE target_table_full_name = 'analytics.gold.daily_revenue'
ORDER BY event_time DESC;
```

1.136.4 Query History

```sql
-- Analyze query performance
SELECT
    start_time,
    end_time,
    duration / 1000 AS duration_seconds,
    statement_type,
    status,
    total_task_duration_ms,
    rows_produced,
    executed_as
FROM system.query.history
WHERE start_time > current_timestamp() - INTERVAL 24 HOURS
  AND duration > 60000 ---queries longer than 1 minute
ORDER BY duration DESC
LIMIT 20;
```

Exam Tip: System tables are accessed through the `system` catalog. Key tables include `system.access.audit` (audit logs), `system.billing.usage` (compute costs), `system.access.table_lineage` (data lineage), and `system.query.history` (query performance). Know what information is available in each.

1.137 Alerting

1.137.1 Job-Level Notifications

```
{
    "email_notifications": {
        "on_start": ["team@company.com"],
        "on_success": ["team@company.com"],
        "on_failure": ["oncall@company.com", "team@company.com"],
        "on_duration_warning_threshold_exceeded": ["oncall@company.com"]
    },
    "health": {
        "rules": [
            {
                "metric": "RUN_DURATION_SECONDS",
                "op": "GREATER_THAN",
                "value": 3600
            }
        ]
    },
    "webhook_notifications": {
        "on_failure": [
            {"id": "webhook-id-for-slack"}
        ]
    }
}
```

1.137.2 SQL Alerts

SQL Alerts monitor query results and trigger notifications when conditions are met:

```
-- Create a query to monitor for data freshness
SELECT
    MAX(order_date) AS latest_order_date,
    DATEDIFF(CURRENT_DATE(), MAX(order_date)) AS days_since_last_order
FROM analytics.silver.orders;
-- Alert condition: days_since_last_order > 1
```

Configuration: 1. Create a SQL query in the SQL editor 2. Click **Create Alert** from the query 3. Set the alert condition (e.g., `days_since_last_order > 1`) 4. Configure notification destinations (email, Slack, PagerDuty) 5. Set the evaluation frequency

1.137.3 Data Quality Alerts

Monitor DLT expectations through the event log:

```
-- Alert when data quality drops below threshold
SELECT
    timestamp,
    details:flow_name::STRING AS dataset,
    details:data_quality.dropped_records::INT AS dropped_records,
    details:data_quality.output_records::INT AS output_records,
    ROUND(
        details:data_quality.dropped_records::FLOAT /
        (details:data_quality.dropped_records::FLOAT +
         details:data_quality.output_records::FLOAT) * 100,
        2
    ) AS drop_rate_pct
FROM event_log(TABLE(analytics.silver_orders))
WHERE event_type = 'flow_progress'
  AND details:data_quality IS NOT NULL
```

```
ORDER BY timestamp DESC;
```

> **Exam Tip:** Know the three notification channels: **email, webhooks** (Slack, Teams), and **SQL Alerts** (query-based monitoring). SQL Alerts are particularly useful for monitoring data freshness, row counts, and data quality metrics on a schedule.

1.138 The Spark UI

The Spark UI is the primary tool for diagnosing performance issues at the execution level.

1.138.1 Key Tabs

Jobs Tab: Shows all Spark jobs triggered by your notebook or task. Each Spark job corresponds to an action (e.g., `count()`, `write()`).

Stages Tab: Each job is broken into stages separated by shuffle boundaries. Shows: - Input/output sizes - Shuffle read/write volumes - Number of tasks - Duration

Tasks Tab: Within each stage, shows individual task metrics: - GC time (garbage collection) - Shuffle read/write per task - Data skew (uneven task durations)

SQL/DataFrame Tab: Shows the physical execution plan for each query, including: - Scan operations - Join strategies (broadcast, sort-merge) - Aggregate operations - Exchange (shuffle) operations

Storage Tab: Shows cached DataFrames and their memory/disk usage.

1.138.2 Reading the DAG Visualization

```
Scan Delta [orders]            Scan Delta [customers]
         |                              |
         └──────── BroadcastExchange ───┘
                          |
              BroadcastHashJoin
                          |
                 HashAggregate
                          |
                    Exchange
                          |
                 HashAggregate
                          |
                 Write Delta
```

Key operations to watch for: - **Exchange** (shuffle): Data redistribution across the cluster. Expensive operation. - **BroadcastExchange:** Distributing a small table to all workers. Much cheaper than shuffle. - **Sort**: Sorting data, often needed before sort-merge joins. - **SortMergeJoin**: Both sides are shuffled and sorted. Expensive. - **BroadcastHashJoin**: Small side is broadcast. Efficient.

> **Exam Tip:** The Spark UI is critical for performance troubleshooting. Know that **Exchange** nodes represent shuffles (expensive), **BroadcastHashJoin** is faster than **SortMergeJoin** for joins with a small table, and uneven task durations in a stage indicate **data skew**.

1.139 Common Performance Issues

1.139.1 Data Skew

Symptom: Most tasks in a stage complete quickly, but a few tasks take much longer.

Cause: Uneven distribution of data across partitions, often caused by a join key or group-by key with hot values (e.g., a disproportionately common customer_id).

Solutions:

```
# Solution 1: Salting the skewed key
from pyspark.sql.functions import concat, lit, rand, floor

# Add a salt to the skewed key
num_salts = 10
salted_large = large_df.withColumn(
    "salted_key",
    concat(col("join_key"), lit("_"), floor(rand() * num_salts).cast("int"))
)

# Explode the small table to match all salts
from pyspark.sql.functions import explode, array

salted_small = small_df.withColumn(
    "salted_key",
    explode(array([concat(col("join_key"), lit(f"_{i}")) for i in range(num_salts)]))
)

result = salted_large.join(salted_small, "salted_key")
```

```
# Solution 2: Enable Adaptive Query Execution (AQE)
spark.conf.set("spark.sql.adaptive.enabled", "true")  # enabled by default
spark.conf.set("spark.sql.adaptive.skewJoin.enabled", "true")
```

1.139.2 Out of Memory (OOM) Errors

Symptom: `java.lang.OutOfMemoryError` or tasks killed by YARN for exceeding memory limits.

Common causes and solutions:

```
# Cause 1: Collecting too much data to the driver
# BAD:
all_data = df.collect()  # Pulls entire DataFrame to driver memory

# GOOD:
sample = df.limit(1000).collect()  # Limit before collecting

# Cause 2: Broadcasting too large a table
# Check broadcast threshold
spark.conf.set("spark.sql.autoBroadcastJoinThreshold", "-1")  # Disable auto-broadcast

# Cause 3: Too few partitions for large data
df = df.repartition(200)  # Increase parallelism

# Cause 4: UDF with large accumulations
# Use Pandas UDFs instead of Python UDFs for better memory management
```

1.139.3 Small Files Problem

Symptom: Slow reads despite small total data volume. Many small Parquet files.

Solutions:

```sql
-- Solution 1: Run OPTIMIZE
OPTIMIZE analytics.silver.orders;

-- Solution 2: Enable auto-optimization
ALTER TABLE analytics.silver.orders SET TBLPROPERTIES (
    'delta.autoOptimize.optimizeWrite' = 'true',
    'delta.autoOptimize.autoCompact' = 'true'
);
```

```python
# Solution 3: Repartition before writing
df.repartition(10).write.format("delta").mode("overwrite") \
    .saveAsTable("analytics.silver.orders")

# Solution 4: Use coalesce for fewer partitions (no shuffle)
df.coalesce(10).write.format("delta").mode("append") \
    .saveAsTable("analytics.silver.orders")
```

1.139.4 Shuffle Spill

Symptom: Stage takes much longer than expected. Spark UI shows "Spill (Memory)" and "Spill (Disk)" metrics.
Cause: Insufficient memory for shuffle operations, causing data to spill to disk.
Solutions:

```python
# Increase shuffle partitions (default is 200)
spark.conf.set("spark.sql.shuffle.partitions", "400")

# Use larger worker nodes with more memory
# Configure in cluster settings

# Enable AQE to auto-coalesce shuffle partitions
spark.conf.set("spark.sql.adaptive.enabled", "true")
spark.conf.set("spark.sql.adaptive.coalescePartitions.enabled", "true")
```

> **Exam Tip:** The four most common performance issues are: **data skew** (uneven partition sizes), **OOM errors** (too much data in memory), **small files** (too many tiny Parquet files), and **shuffle spill** (insufficient memory for shuffles). Know the symptoms and solutions for each.

1.140 Adaptive Query Execution (AQE)

AQE dynamically optimizes query plans at runtime based on actual data statistics:

1.140.1 AQE Features

```python
# AQE is enabled by default in Databricks Runtime 14+
spark.conf.set("spark.sql.adaptive.enabled", "true")

# Key AQE features:
# Coalescing post-shuffle partitions (reduces small partitions)
spark.conf.set("spark.sql.adaptive.coalescePartitions.enabled", "true")

# Converting sort-merge joins to broadcast joins
spark.conf.set("spark.sql.adaptive.localShuffleReader.enabled", "true")

# Optimizing skew joins
```

```
spark.conf.set("spark.sql.adaptive.skewJoin.enabled", "true")
spark.conf.set("spark.sql.adaptive.skewJoin.skewedPartitionFactor", "5")
spark.conf.set("spark.sql.adaptive.skewJoin.skewedPartitionThresholdInBytes", "256m")
```

1.140.2 How AQE Handles Skew

1. After a shuffle, AQE detects partitions significantly larger than the median
2. It automatically splits skewed partitions into smaller sub-partitions
3. Each sub-partition is processed by a separate task
4. Results are combined transparently

> **Exam Tip:** AQE is enabled by default in Databricks and provides automatic optimization for three common problems: coalescing small post-shuffle partitions, converting sort-merge joins to broadcast joins when one side is smaller than expected, and handling skewed joins. Know that AQE operates at runtime, not at compile time.

1.141 Troubleshooting DLT Pipelines

1.141.1 DLT Event Log Queries

```sql
-- View recent pipeline events
SELECT
    id,
    timestamp,
    level,
    event_type,
    message
FROM event_log(TABLE(analytics.silver_orders))
ORDER BY timestamp DESC
LIMIT 50;

-- Check data quality expectation results
SELECT
    timestamp,
    details:flow_name::STRING AS dataset_name,
    details:data_quality.num_output_rows::INT AS output_rows,
    details:data_quality.num_expected_records::INT AS expected_records,
    expectation.name AS expectation_name,
    expectation.dataset AS dataset,
    expectation.passed_records AS passed,
    expectation.failed_records AS failed
FROM event_log(TABLE(analytics.silver_orders)),
LATERAL VIEW EXPLODE(
    from_json(
        details:data_quality:expectations,
        'ARRAY<STRUCT<name:STRING,dataset:STRING,passed_records:INT,failed_records:INT>>'
    )
) AS expectation
WHERE event_type = 'flow_progress'
ORDER BY timestamp DESC;
```

1.141.2 Common DLT Issues

Issue	Cause	Solution
Pipeline fails on start	Syntax error in notebook	Check error message in event log
Schema mismatch	Source schema changed	Enable schema evolution or update DDL
Expectation failure	`expect_or_fail` constraint violated	Fix source data or relax to `expect_or_drop`
Slow performance	Too many small files in source	Use Auto Loader instead of listing files
State corruption	Checkpoint incompatible with code change	Perform a full refresh of the pipeline

1.141.3 Full Refresh vs. Incremental Update

```
{
    "task_key": "run_pipeline",
    "pipeline_task": {
        "pipeline_id": "pipeline-id",
        "full_refresh": true
    }
}
```

- **Incremental update** (default): Only processes new data since the last run
- **Full refresh**: Reprocesses all data from scratch, recreating all tables

Use full refresh when: - Pipeline logic has changed significantly - Checkpoints are corrupted - Schema changes are incompatible with existing data - You need to backfill historical data

---

1.142 Logging Best Practices

1.142.1 Structured Logging in Notebooks

```python
import logging

logger = logging.getLogger("etl_pipeline")
logger.setLevel(logging.INFO)

# Log pipeline metrics
logger.info(f"Ingested {row_count} rows from {source_path}")
logger.info(f"Transformation complete: {output_count} rows, {rejected_count} rejected")
logger.warning(f"Data quality: {error_rate:.1%} error rate exceeds 5% threshold")
logger.error(f"Failed to write to {target_table}: {str(e)}")
```

1.142.2 Custom Metrics with Task Values

```python
# Store pipeline metrics as task values for monitoring
dbutils.jobs.taskValues.set(key="rows_ingested", value=ingested_count)
dbutils.jobs.taskValues.set(key="rows_transformed", value=transformed_count)
dbutils.jobs.taskValues.set(key="rows_rejected", value=rejected_count)
dbutils.jobs.taskValues.set(key="error_rate", value=round(error_rate, 4))
dbutils.jobs.taskValues.set(key="duration_seconds", value=duration)
```

1.142.3 Data Freshness Monitoring

```
-- Monitor data freshness across tables
SELECT
    table_catalog,
    table_schema,
    table_name,
    last_altered AS last_updated,
    TIMESTAMPDIFF(HOUR, last_altered, CURRENT_TIMESTAMP()) AS hours_since_update
FROM system.information_schema.tables
WHERE table_schema IN ('bronze', 'silver', 'gold')
ORDER BY hours_since_update DESC;
```

1.143 Chapter Summary

In this chapter, you learned:

- Monitor pipelines through the **Workflows UI, Spark UI, system tables**, and **DLT event log**
- **System tables** provide queryable audit logs, billing data, lineage, and query history
- **SQL Alerts** monitor query results and trigger notifications for data quality or freshness issues
- The **Spark UI** helps diagnose performance issues through DAG visualization and task-level metrics
- Common performance problems: **data skew, OOM errors, small files**, and **shuffle spill**
- **Adaptive Query Execution (AQE)** automatically optimizes queries at runtime
- DLT pipelines are monitored through the **event log**, which captures data quality expectation metrics
- **Full refresh** reprocesses all data; **incremental update** processes only new data

---

1.144 Practice Questions

Question 1: A data engineer notices that most tasks in a Spark stage complete in 2 seconds, but three tasks take over 10 minutes. What is the most likely cause?

A. Insufficient cluster memory B. Data skew in the partition keys C. Network latency between worker nodes D. Disk I/O bottleneck

Question 2: Which system table provides information about compute costs and DBU consumption?

A. `system.access.audit` B. `system.billing.usage` C. `system.query.history` D. `system.access.table_lineage`

Question 3: A streaming pipeline's state is growing unboundedly, causing increasing memory usage. What is the most likely missing configuration?

A. Checkpoint location B. Watermark C. Trigger interval D. Output mode

Question 4: Which Spark UI metric indicates that data is being spilled from memory to disk during a shuffle?

A. GC Time B. Shuffle Read Size C. Spill (Disk) D. Input Size

Question 5: A DLT pipeline uses `@dlt.expect` expectations. Where can the data engineer view how many records passed and failed each expectation?

A. The Delta Lake transaction log B. The DLT event log C. The Spark UI SQL tab D. The Unity Catalog audit log

Question 6: Which AQE feature automatically splits oversized partitions to handle data skew?

A. Coalescing post-shuffle partitions B. Converting sort-merge joins to broadcast joins C. Optimizing skew joins D. Partition pruning

Question 7: A data engineer wants to be notified when a gold table has not been updated in over 24 hours. Which approach is MOST appropriate?

A. Configure a job-level email notification B. Create a SQL Alert that checks the table's last update timestamp C. Enable audit logging on the table D. Add a DLT expectation to the pipeline

Question 8: Which operation in the Spark UI DAG visualization represents a data shuffle?

A. Scan B. Filter C. Exchange D. Project

Question 9: What is the primary benefit of using `coalesce()` instead of `repartition()` to reduce the number of partitions?

A. `coalesce()` supports increasing the number of partitions B. `coalesce()` avoids a full shuffle by combining existing partitions C. `coalesce()` produces more evenly distributed partitions D. `coalesce()` is faster because it skips the write step

Question 10: A job run has the state TERMINATED with result_state TIMED_OUT. What happened?

A. The cluster ran out of memory B. The job exceeded its configured timeout duration C. The network connection to the workspace was lost D. The job was manually cancelled by an administrator

---

1.145 Answer Explanations

Question 1: B. When most tasks complete quickly but a few take disproportionately longer, the most likely cause is data skew—some partitions contain significantly more data than others. The slow tasks are processing the oversized partitions. Reference: Spark data skew troubleshooting guide.

Question 2: B. The `system.billing.usage` table provides information about DBU consumption, compute costs, SKU types, and associated cluster/job IDs. Reference: Databricks system tables documentation.

Question 3: B. Without a watermark, Spark must maintain aggregation state for all possible keys indefinitely, leading to unbounded state growth. A watermark tells Spark when it is safe to discard old state. Reference: Structured Streaming state management.

Question 4: C. "Spill (Disk)" in the Spark UI indicates that data is being spilled from memory to disk during operations like shuffles, sorts, or aggregations. This slows performance significantly. Reference: Spark UI metrics documentation.

Question 5: B. The DLT event log captures data quality metrics, including the number of records that passed and failed each expectation constraint. This is the primary monitoring tool for DLT data quality. Reference: DLT event log documentation.

Question 6: C. AQE's skew join optimization detects partitions significantly larger than the median after a shuffle and automatically splits them into smaller sub-partitions for parallel processing. Reference: Spark AQE documentation.

Question 7: B. A SQL Alert can run a query on a schedule that checks the table's last update timestamp and triggers a notification when the staleness threshold is exceeded. Job-level notifications only report on job outcomes, not data freshness. Reference: Databricks SQL Alerts documentation.

Question 8: C. An Exchange node in the Spark DAG represents a data shuffle—the redistribution of data across partitions. Shuffles are expensive operations that move data between workers. Reference: Spark execution plan documentation.

Question 9: B. `coalesce()` reduces partitions by merging existing partitions on the same worker without a full data shuffle. `repartition()` performs a full shuffle to evenly redistribute data. `coalesce()` is more efficient when reducing partition count. Reference: PySpark coalesce vs repartition documentation.

Question 10: B. The TIMED_OUT result state indicates that the job exceeded its configured `timeout_seconds` value and was automatically terminated. This is different from manual cancellation (CANCELED) or memory errors (FAILED). Reference: Databricks job run states documentation. # Chapter 15: Practice Exams

Meridian Certification Press—Microsoft DP-750: Implementing Azure Databricks Study Guide 2026

1.146 How to Use These Practice Exams

This chapter contains three full-length practice exams, each with 40 questions. These exams are designed to simulate the DP-750 exam experience in terms of difficulty, question types, and domain coverage.

Recommended approach:

1. Set a timer for 80 minutes per exam (the real exam allows 120 minutes for 40-60 questions)
2. Do not reference this guide or external materials during the exam
3. Record your answers before checking the answer key

4. Score yourself: each question is worth 2.5 points (40 questions = 100 points)
5. A score of 70% or above indicates readiness for the real exam
6. Review all incorrect answers and study the referenced topics before attempting the next practice exam

Domain distribution per exam:

Domain	Weight	Questions per Exam
Domain 1: Implement and manage a lakehouse	25-30%	10-12
Domain 2: Transform data	25-30%	10-12
Domain 3: Manage and monitor data pipelines	20-25%	8-10
Domain 4: Design and implement security	15-20%	6-8

2

Practice Exam 1

2.1 Questions

Question 1. A data engineer creates a Delta table with the following command:

```
CREATE TABLE analytics.sales.transactions (
    txn_id BIGINT NOT NULL,
    amount DECIMAL(10,2),
    txn_date DATE,
    txn_year INT GENERATED ALWAYS AS (YEAR(txn_date))
)
USING DELTA;
```

What happens when a row is inserted with `txn_date = '2026-03-15'` and `txn_year = 2025`?

A. The row is inserted with `txn_year = 2025` as specified B. The row is inserted with `txn_year = 2026`, overriding the provided value C. The insert fails because generated columns cannot be explicitly set D. The row is inserted with both values stored, but queries return 2026

Question 2. A streaming pipeline reads from a Delta table and writes to another Delta table. The pipeline uses `trigger(availableNow=True)`. Which statement is true?

A. The pipeline runs continuously, processing micro-batches as data arrives B. The pipeline processes all available data in a single micro-batch and stops C. The pipeline processes all available data across multiple micro-batches and stops D. The pipeline processes one micro-batch and stops, even if more data is available

Question 3. A data engineer needs to create a Unity Catalog external table that reads data from an ADLS Gen2 container. Which objects must exist before the external table can be created? (Select all that apply.)

A. A storage credential B. An external location mapped to the ADLS Gen2 path C. A managed identity assigned to the Databricks workspace D. A Delta Live Tables pipeline E. A catalog and schema for the table

Question 4. Which command compacts small files in a Delta table and co-locates data based on frequently filtered columns?

A. `VACUUM analytics.sales.orders ZORDER BY (order_date);` B. `OPTIMIZE analytics.sales.orders ZORDER BY (order_date );` C. `ALTER TABLE analytics.sales.orders CLUSTER BY (order_date);` D. `COMPACT TABLE analytics.sales.orders SORT BY (order_date);`

Question 5. A data engineer configures Auto Loader to ingest JSON files from a cloud storage directory. The schema of the incoming files may change over time. Which Auto Loader option enables automatic handling of schema changes?

A. `cloudFiles.format` B. `cloudFiles.schemaLocation` C. `cloudFiles.inferColumnTypes` D. `cloudFiles.schemaEvolutionMode`

Question 6. A Delta Live Tables pipeline has the following definition:

```
@dlt.table(
    comment="Cleaned customer data"
)
@dlt.expect_or_drop("valid_email", "email IS NOT NULL AND email LIKE '%@%'")
@dlt.expect("valid_age", "age BETWEEN 0 AND 150")
def silver_customers():
    return dlt.read("bronze_customers").select("*")
```

A record arrives with `email = NULL` and `age = 200`. What happens to this record?

A. The record is dropped because `valid_email` fails B. The record is dropped because both expectations fail C. The record is inserted because `valid_age` uses `expect` (warn only) D. The record is inserted with `email = NULL` and `age = 200`

Question 7. A Databricks Workflow has the following task dependency graph:

```
Task A ⟶ Task B ⟶ Task D
Task A ⟶ Task C ⟶ Task D
```

Task B fails. What is the default behavior?

A. Task C continues; Task D runs only if Task C succeeds B. Task C continues; Task D is skipped because Task B failed C. Task C is cancelled because it shares a dependency with Task B D. The entire workflow is immediately cancelled

Question 8. Which statement about Unity Catalog metastores is correct?

A. Each workspace must have its own dedicated metastore B. A metastore can span multiple Azure regions C. A metastore is shared across all workspaces in the same Azure region D. Metastores are automatically created when a workspace is deployed

Question 9. A data engineer runs the following query:

```
SELECT * FROM analytics.silver.orders VERSION AS OF 15;
```

The table is currently at version 22. VACUUM was last run with `RETAIN 168 HOURS`, and version 15 was committed 5 days ago. What is the result?

A. The query returns data as of version 15 B. The query fails because version 15 has been vacuumed C. The query returns current data (version 22) because VACUUM removes old versions D. The query fails because VERSION AS OF requires a timestamp, not a version number

Question 10. A data engineer needs to create a Structured Streaming query that performs a windowed aggregation (count of events per 5-minute window) and writes results to a Delta table only after the window is finalized. Which combination of features is required?

A. Tumbling window + watermark + append output mode B. Tumbling window + complete output mode C. Sliding window + watermark + update output mode D. Session window + append output mode (no watermark needed)

Question 11. What is the default checkpoint interval for the Delta Lake transaction log?

A. Every commit B. Every 5 commits C. Every 10 commits D. Every 100 commits

Question 12. A data engineer needs to ingest data from a Kafka topic into a Delta table. The Kafka messages contain JSON payloads. Which function should be used to parse the Kafka value column?

A. `parse_json()` B. `from_json()` C. `json_decode()` D. `json_extract()`

Question 13. Which Delta table property enables automatic compaction of small files after write operations?

A. `delta.autoOptimize.autoCompact` B. `delta.autoOptimize.optimizeWrite` C. `delta.autoCompaction.enabled` D. `delta.smallFileCompaction`

Question 14. A Databricks job is configured with a retry policy of `max_retries = 3` on a task. The task fails on the first attempt, succeeds on the second attempt. How many total attempts were made?

A. 1 B. 2 C. 3 D. 4

Question 15. A data engineer applies a row filter to a table so that members of the `us-team` group can only see rows where `country = 'US'`. A member of `us-team` creates a view on top of this table. What does a user outside of `us-team` see when querying the view?

A. All rows, because the view bypasses the row filter B. Only US rows, because the row filter is enforced regardless of access method C. No rows, because they cannot access the underlying table D. An error, because views cannot be created on tables with row filters

Question 16. Which command shows the history of all operations performed on a Delta table?

A. `SHOW HISTORY analytics.sales.orders;` B. `DESCRIBE HISTORY analytics.sales.orders;` C. `SELECT * FROM analytics.sales.orders._delta_log;` D. `DESCRIBE DETAIL analytics.sales.orders;`

Question 17. A data engineer needs to process all files that have arrived since the last pipeline run. The pipeline should process data across multiple efficient micro-batches and then stop. Which streaming trigger should they use?

A. `trigger(once=True)` B. `trigger(availableNow=True)` C. `trigger(processingTime="0 seconds")` D. Default trigger (no trigger specification)

Question 18. In Unity Catalog, what is the correct three-level namespace for referencing a table?

A. `workspace.database.table` B. `metastore.schema.table` C. `catalog.schema.table` D. `database.schema.table`

Question 19. A data engineer writes data to a Delta table using PySpark with `mode("append")`. The incoming DataFrame has an extra column not present in the target table. Schema evolution is not enabled. What happens?

A. The extra column is silently dropped B. The extra column is added to the table automatically C. The write fails with a schema mismatch error D. The extra column values are stored but not queryable

Question 20. Which Spark UI tab is most useful for diagnosing data skew in a join operation?

A. SQL tab B. Storage tab C. Stages tab (task-level metrics) D. Environment tab

Question 21. A data engineer uses `MERGE INTO` to upsert records. The source table has 1,000 rows: 800 match existing records in the target, and 200 are new. The MERGE statement has `WHEN MATCHED THEN UPDATE` and `WHEN NOT MATCHED THEN INSERT` clauses. How many rows are affected?

A. 200 (only inserts) B. 800 (only updates) C. 1,000 (800 updates + 200 inserts) D. 1,800 (800 updates create new versions + 200 inserts + 800 original rows)

Question 22. A data engineer needs to create a Feature Store table with time-series features. The features should support point-in-time lookups. Which parameter must be specified when creating the feature table?

A. `partition_columns` B. `timestamp_keys` C. `time_travel_enabled` D. `temporal_join_key`

Question 23. Which DLT expectation decorator drops records that violate the data quality rule?

A. `@dlt.expect` B. `@dlt.expect_or_drop` C. `@dlt.expect_or_fail` D. `@dlt.expect_and_remove`

Question 24. A data engineer needs to share data with an external organization without giving them access to the Databricks workspace. Which feature supports this?

A. Unity Catalog external tables B. Delta Sharing C. Azure Private Link D. Service principal authentication

Question 25. A streaming query writes to a Delta table using append output mode. The checkpoint location is accidentally deleted. What happens when the query restarts?

A. The query resumes from the last committed offset B. The query reprocesses all data from the beginning C. The query fails with a checkpoint not found error D. The query creates a new checkpoint and skips all existing data

Question 26. Which MLflow function creates a Spark UDF from a registered model for efficient batch inference on a DataFrame?

A. `mlflow.pyfunc.load_model()` B. `mlflow.pyfunc.spark_udf()` C. `mlflow.spark.create_udf()` D. `mlflow.models.to_spark()`

Question 27. A data engineer configures a Databricks Workflow to run daily at 8:00 AM. On Monday, the job takes 3 hours to complete. On Tuesday, the job is still running when the next scheduled run (8:00 AM) triggers. What is the default behavior?

A. The scheduled run is skipped B. The scheduled run starts a new concurrent execution C. The running job is cancelled and the new run starts D. The scheduled run is queued and starts after the current run finishes

Question 28. What is the purpose of the `delta.dataSkippingNumIndexedCols` table property?

A. It sets the maximum number of columns allowed in the table B. It controls how many columns have min/max statistics collected for data skipping C. It limits the number of columns that can be used in Z-ORDER D. It determines how many columns are included in the checkpoint files

Question 29. A data engineer needs to grant a service principal permission to read all current and future tables in a schema. Which GRANT statement achieves this?

A. `GRANT SELECT ON ALL TABLES IN SCHEMA analytics.silver TO 'etl-sp';` B. `GRANT SELECT ON SCHEMA analytics.silver TO 'etl-sp';` C. `GRANT READ ON SCHEMA analytics.silver TO 'etl-sp';` D. `GRANT ALL PRIVILEGES ON SCHEMA analytics.silver TO 'etl-sp';`

Question 30. A Delta Live Tables pipeline has a materialized view and a streaming table. Which statement is correct?

A. Both are append-only and cannot handle updates B. Materialized views support full recomputation; streaming tables are append-only C. Streaming tables support full recomputation; materialized views are append-only D. Both support full recomputation and incremental updates interchangeably

Question 31. A data engineer discovers that a Structured Streaming query's state store is growing unboundedly. The query performs a `groupBy().count()` aggregation. What is the most likely cause?

A. The query is using complete output mode instead of append B. The query does not have a watermark defined C. The checkpoint location is on local disk instead of cloud storage D. The query is reading too many files per trigger

Question 32. Which Azure Databricks feature should be used to prevent users from creating clusters with more than 10 worker nodes?

A. Unity Catalog permissions B. Cluster policies C. Network Security Groups D. Azure resource locks

Question 33. A data engineer runs the following Auto Loader configuration:

```
stream_df = (spark.readStream
    .format("cloudFiles")
    .option("cloudFiles.format", "csv")
    .option("cloudFiles.schemaLocation", "/checkpoints/schema/")
    .option("cloudFiles.schemaHints", "amount DECIMAL(10,2), txn_date DATE")
    .load("/Volumes/raw/transactions/"))
```

What is the purpose of `schemaHints`?

A. It defines the complete schema, overriding schema inference B. It provides type hints for specific columns while allowing Auto Loader to infer the rest C. It validates incoming data against the specified types D. It specifies the schema for the checkpoint files

Question 34. A data engineer needs to create a MERGE statement that: (1) updates matching records, (2) inserts non-matching records, and (3) deletes matched records where the source has `is_deleted = true`. How many `WHEN MATCHED` clauses are needed?

A. 1 B. 2 C. 3 D. MERGE does not support DELETE operations

Question 35. Which type of network connectivity ensures that traffic between a Databricks cluster and Azure Data Lake Storage never traverses the public internet?

A. VNet injection B. Azure Private Endpoints C. IP access lists D. Customer-managed encryption keys

Question 36. A data engineer creates a Delta table with `CLUSTER BY (region, order_date)`. After several days of data ingestion, they run `OPTIMIZE` on the table. What optimization technique is applied?

A. Z-ORDER on the specified columns B. Liquid Clustering on the specified columns C. Partitioning by the specified columns D. Standard file compaction without clustering

Question 37. A streaming pipeline uses the Change Data Feed (CDF) to capture row-level changes from a source table. A record in the source is updated. How many CDF records are produced for this single update?

A. 1 record with `_change_type = 'update'` B. 2 records: `update_preimage` and `update_postimage` C. 3 records: `delete`, `insert`, and `update` D. 1 record with the new values and a `_commit_version` column

Question 38. A data engineer needs to ensure that a column in a Delta table never contains negative values. Which constraint should they apply?

A. `NOT NULL` constraint B. `UNIQUE` constraint C. `CHECK` constraint D. `DEFAULT` constraint

Question 39. Which system table should a data engineer query to see which users accessed a specific table and when?

A. `system.information_schema.tables` B. `system.access.audit` C. `system.billing.usage` D. `system.access.table_lineage`

Question 40. A data engineer deploys an MLflow model to a Model Serving endpoint with two versions: version 5 (90% traffic) and version 6 (10% traffic). After monitoring shows version 6 performs better, the engineer wants to route all traffic to version 6. What should they do?

A. Delete version 5 from the model registry B. Update the traffic configuration to route 100% to version 6 C. Create a new serving endpoint with only version 6 D. Set the "champion" alias to version 6 (the endpoint automatically follows aliases)

2.2 Practice Exam 1—Answer Key

Question 1: C. Generated columns defined with `GENERATED ALWAYS AS` cannot be explicitly set during insertion. The insert will fail with an error. If you want to allow explicit values, use `GENERATED BY DEFAULT AS`. Reference: Chapter 4, Section 4.9.3.

Question 2: C. `trigger(availableNow=True)` processes all available data across multiple efficient micro-batches and then stops. This differs from `trigger(once=True)`, which processes all data in a single micro-batch. Reference: Chapter 9, Section 9.5.3.

Question 3: A, B, E. To create an external table, you need: (1) a storage credential for authentication, (2) an external location mapping the UC path to the cloud storage URL, and (3) a catalog and schema to contain the table. A managed identity may be used by the storage credential but is not a separate requirement. DLT is unrelated. Reference: Chapter 3 and Chapter 14, Section 14.10.

Question 4: B. `OPTIMIZE ... ZORDER BY` compacts small files and co-locates data using Z-ORDER. VACUUM removes old files but does not compact. `CLUSTER BY` is for Liquid Clustering (specified at table creation). `COMPACT TABLE` is not a valid command. Reference: Chapter 4, Section 4.7.

Question 5: D. `cloudFiles.schemaEvolutionMode` controls how Auto Loader handles schema changes (options include `addNewColumns`, `rescue`, `failOnNewColumns`, `none`). `schemaLocation` stores the inferred schema but does not control evolution behavior. Reference: Chapter 6.

Question 6: A. The record is dropped because the `email` fails the `expect_or_drop` expectation. The `expect_or_drop` decorator drops any record that violates the rule. The `valid_age` expectation uses `expect` (warn only), which would log a warning but not drop the record. However, since `expect_or_drop` already drops the record before `expect` evaluates, the record never reaches the table. Reference: Chapter 10.

Question 7: B. By default, when a task fails, independent parallel tasks continue running, but downstream tasks that depend on the failed task are skipped. Task C continues because it depends only on Task A (which succeeded). Task D is skipped because it depends on both Task B (failed) and Task C. Reference: Chapter 11.

Question 8: C. A Unity Catalog metastore is created per Azure region and shared across all workspaces assigned to it in that region. A metastore cannot span multiple regions. Metastores must be explicitly created and assigned. Reference: Chapter 3, Section 3.2.

Question 9: A. The query returns data as of version 15. VACUUM with `RETAIN 168 HOURS` (7 days) removes files older than 7 days. Since version 15 was committed 5 days ago, its data files have not been vacuumed yet. Time travel works for any version whose data files still exist. Reference: Chapter 4, Section 4.6.

Question 10: A. To write windowed aggregation results only after the window is finalized, you need: (1) a tumbling window for fixed-period aggregation, (2) a watermark to define when windows are considered final, and (3) append output mode, which emits results only when the watermark passes the window's end time. Reference: Chapter 9, Sections 9.6 and 9.7.

Question 11: C. Delta Lake creates checkpoint files in the transaction log every 10 commits by default. Checkpoints consolidate the log state into Parquet format for efficient reads. Reference: Chapter 4, Section 4.2.2.

Question 12: B. `from_json()` is the PySpark function used to parse a JSON string column into a structured column using a specified schema. Kafka message values are binary and must be cast to string first, then parsed with `from_json()`. Reference: Chapter 9, Section 9.2.3.

Question 13: A. `delta.autoOptimize.autoCompact` enables automatic compaction of small files after write operations. `delta.autoOptimize.optimizeWrite` coalesces files during writes (preventing small files) but does not compact existing ones. Reference: Chapter 4, Section 4.10.

Question 14: B. The task runs once (fails), then retries once (succeeds), for a total of 2 attempts. The `max_retries = 3` means up to 3 additional attempts after the initial attempt (4 total), but the task succeeded on the first retry. Reference: Chapter 11.

Question 15: B. Row filters are enforced at the Unity Catalog level regardless of how the data is accessed—including through views. The `us-team` member's view does not bypass the filter. Users outside `us-team` querying the view would see results according to their own row filter evaluation. Reference: Chapter 14, Section 14.4.

Question 16: B. `DESCRIBE HISTORY` shows the complete history of all operations (writes, updates, deletes, merges, optimizes) performed on a Delta table, including version numbers, timestamps, and operation details. Reference: Chapter 4, Section 4.6.3.

Question 17: B. `trigger(availableNow=True)` processes all available data across multiple micro-batches and then stops. It is the recommended approach for scheduled batch-style processing of streaming sources. Reference: Chapter 9, Section 9.5.3.

Question 18: C. Unity Catalog uses the three-level namespace `catalog.schema.table`. Catalogs are the top-level grouping, schemas (also called databases) are within catalogs, and tables are within schemas. Reference: Chapter 3, Section 3.2.

Question 19: C. Delta Lake enforces schema on write by default. If the incoming DataFrame has columns not present in the target table, the write fails with a schema mismatch error. To allow new columns, use `.option("mergeSchema", "true")`. Reference: Chapter 4, Section 4.8.

Question 20: C. The Stages tab in the Spark UI shows task-level metrics including task duration, input/output sizes, and shuffle read/write sizes. Data skew appears as a few tasks taking much longer than others or processing much more data. Reference: Chapter 12.

Question 21: C. The MERGE affects all 1,000 source rows: 800 are matched and updated, 200 are not matched and inserted, for a total of 1,000 rows affected. The operation is atomic. Reference: Chapter 4, Section 4.5.3.

Question 22: B. The `timestamp_keys` parameter enables point-in-time lookups in Feature Store tables, ensuring that during training, only feature values available at or before each training example's timestamp are used. Reference: Chapter 13, Section 13.5.5.

Question 23: B. `@dlt.expect_or_drop` drops records that violate the expectation. `@dlt.expect` logs a warning but keeps the record. `@dlt.expect_or_fail` causes the pipeline to fail. Reference: Chapter 10.

Question 24: B. Delta Sharing is an open protocol for securely sharing data with external organizations without requiring them to have access to the Databricks workspace. Recipients can access shared data using any client that supports the Delta Sharing protocol. Reference: Chapter 3.

Question 25: B. Without a checkpoint, the streaming query has no record of what data has been processed. It will reprocess all available data from the beginning of the source. Reference: Chapter 9, Section 9.9.

Question 26: B. `mlflow.pyfunc.spark_udf()` creates a Spark UDF from an MLflow model, enabling distributed batch inference across a Spark cluster. `load_model()` loads the model into the driver only. Reference: Chapter 13, Section 13.7.1.

Question 27: A. By default, if a job run is still executing when the next scheduled trigger occurs, the scheduled run is skipped. This prevents resource contention and duplicate processing. This behavior can be changed using the `max_concurrent_runs` setting. Reference: Chapter 11.

Question 28: B. `delta.dataSkippingNumIndexedCols` controls how many leading columns in the table have min/max statistics collected in the transaction log. These statistics enable data skipping, allowing Spark to skip files that do not contain relevant data for a query's filter conditions. Default is 32. Reference: Chapter 4, Section 4.10.

Question 29: B. `GRANT SELECT ON SCHEMA` grants SELECT permission on all current and future tables within the schema. This is schema-level inheritance. `GRANT SELECT ON ALL TABLES IN SCHEMA` would only apply to current tables (if it were valid syntax). Reference: Chapter 14, Section 14.3.3.

Question 30: B. In Delta Live Tables, materialized views support full recomputation—the entire result is recalculated on each pipeline run. Streaming tables are append-only and process only new data incrementally. Reference: Chapter 10.

Question 31: B. Without a watermark, Spark must maintain aggregation state for all groups indefinitely because it cannot determine when a group is "complete." Adding a watermark allows Spark to drop state for groups that are past the watermark threshold. Reference: Chapter 9, Section 9.6.

Question 32: B. Cluster policies allow workspace administrators to define constraints on cluster configurations, including maximum worker count, allowed instance types, and required tags. Reference: Chapter 14, Section 14.9.

Question 33: B. `schemaHints` provides type hints for specific columns while allowing Auto Loader to infer the types of remaining columns. This is useful when Auto Loader's type inference produces incorrect types (e.g., inferring a decimal as string). Reference: Chapter 6.

Question 34: B. Two `WHEN MATCHED` clauses are needed: one with a condition for deletion (`WHEN MATCHED AND source.is_deleted = true THEN DELETE`) and one for updates (`WHEN MATCHED THEN UPDATE SET ...`). The delete clause must come first (more specific condition). Reference: Chapter 4, Section 4.5.3.

Question 35: B. Azure Private Endpoints ensure that traffic between Databricks clusters and Azure services stays on the Azure private network. VNet injection places clusters in your VNet but does not guarantee private connectivity to storage services. Reference: Chapter 14, Section 14.6.2.

Question 36: B. `CLUSTER BY` at table creation enables Liquid Clustering. Running `OPTIMIZE` on a liquid-clustered table triggers the clustering operation on the specified columns. This is different from Z-ORDER, which is specified as part of the OPTIMIZE command itself. Reference: Chapter 4, Section 4.7.4.

Question 37: B. For each update, Change Data Feed produces two records: `update_preimage` (the row before the change) and `update_postimage` (the row after the change). This allows downstream consumers to see both the old and new values. Reference: Chapter 9, Section 9.11.

Question 38: C. A `CHECK` constraint validates that column values meet a specified condition. For example: `ALTER TABLE t ADD CONSTRAINT positive_amount CHECK (amount >= 0)`. `NOT NULL` only prevents null values. Delta Lake does not support `UNIQUE` constraints. Reference: Chapter 4, Section 4.9.1.

Question 39: B. `system.access.audit` contains detailed audit records of user actions including data access events. `system.access.table_lineage` shows data flow between tables but not individual user access events. Reference: Chapter 14, Section 14.8.

Question 40: B. The simplest approach is to update the traffic configuration to route 100% of traffic to version 6. Deleting version 5 from the registry is unnecessary and removes valuable history. Creating a new endpoint causes downtime. Aliases manage registry-level designations, not serving endpoint routing directly. Reference: Chapter 13, Section 13.6.4.

3

Practice Exam 2

3.1 Questions

Question 1. A data engineer needs to schedule a pipeline that runs every weekday at 6:00 AM and sends an email notification on failure. Which Databricks feature should they use?

A. Delta Live Tables with continuous mode B. Databricks Workflows with a cron schedule and email notifications C. Structured Streaming with a trigger interval D. A notebook with a `time.sleep()` loop

Question 2. Which statement about managed tables in Unity Catalog is correct?

A. Managed tables store data in a location specified by the user B. When a managed table is dropped, the underlying data files are deleted C. Managed tables do not support Delta format D. Managed tables cannot be shared via Delta Sharing

Question 3. A data engineer writes the following PySpark code:

```
df = (spark.readStream
    .format("delta")
    .option("maxFilesPerTrigger", 10)
    .table("analytics.bronze.events"))
```

What does `maxFilesPerTrigger` control?

A. The maximum number of output files written per trigger B. The maximum number of input files processed per micro-batch C. The maximum number of triggers before the stream stops D. The maximum file size in bytes per trigger

Question 4. A Delta table was created with partitioning:

```
CREATE TABLE analytics.sales.orders (
    order_id BIGINT,
    amount DECIMAL(10,2),
    order_date DATE,
    region STRING
)
PARTITIONED BY (region);
```

A query filters on `order_date` but not on `region`. What is the impact?

A. The query reads all partitions, which may be inefficient B. The query automatically uses data skipping on `order_date` C. The query fails because the partition column is not in the WHERE clause D. The query reads only the default partition

Question 5. A data engineer needs to implement column-level security so that the `salary` column in an employee table shows actual values only to HR team members and `NULL` to everyone else. Which approach should they use?

A. Create a separate table for each team with different columns B. Apply a column mask function on the `salary` column C. Use a cluster policy to restrict access D. Remove the `salary` column and create a view

Question 6. What is the minimum retention period that VACUUM will accept by default (without overriding the safety check)?

A. 24 hours B. 48 hours C. 168 hours (7 days) D. 720 hours (30 days)

Question 7. A data engineer is using Databricks AutoML. Which of the following problem types does AutoML support? (Select all that apply.)

A. Classification B. Regression C. Clustering D. Forecasting E. Anomaly detection

Question 8. A Delta Live Tables pipeline uses the following expectation:

```
@dlt.expect_or_fail("positive_amount", "amount > 0")
```

A record with `amount = -5` arrives. What happens?

A. The record is dropped and the pipeline continues B. The record is quarantined in a separate table C. The pipeline fails immediately D. The record is inserted with a warning flag

Question 9. A data engineer creates a secret scope backed by Azure Key Vault. A notebook uses `dbutils.secrets.get(scope="kv-scope", key="db-password")` to retrieve a secret. What appears in the notebook output when the secret value is displayed?

A. The actual password in plain text B. `[REDACTED]` C. An encrypted version of the password D. An error, because secrets cannot be displayed

Question 10. Which command restores a Delta table to a previous version?

A. `ROLLBACK TABLE analytics.sales.orders TO VERSION 5;` B. `RESTORE TABLE analytics.sales.orders TO VERSION AS OF 5;` C. `UNDO analytics.sales.orders VERSION 5;` D. `ALTER TABLE analytics.sales.orders REVERT TO 5;`

Question 11. A Structured Streaming query joins two streams. Which requirements must be met? (Select all that apply.)

A. Both streams must have watermarks defined B. The join condition must include a time constraint C. Both streams must use the same output mode D. Both streams must read from the same source type

Question 12. A data engineer runs `DESCRIBE DETAIL analytics.silver.orders`. Which information is NOT included in the output?

A. Table format (Delta) B. Number of files C. Table size in bytes D. Query execution plan

Question 13. A data engineer needs to pass a value from one task to another in a Databricks Workflow. Which method should they use?

A. Write the value to a shared file in DBFS B. Use `dbutils.jobs.taskValues.set()` and `dbutils.jobs.taskValues.get()` C. Use Spark configuration variables D. Store the value in a Delta table

Question 14. In a Unity Catalog environment, which cluster access mode enforces Unity Catalog permissions for all users on the cluster?

A. Single User mode B. Shared mode C. No Isolation Shared mode D. Both Single User and Shared modes

Question 15. A data engineer wants to use schema evolution with Auto Loader so that new columns in incoming files are automatically added to the target table. Which `schemaEvolutionMode` setting achieves this?

A. `rescue` B. `failOnNewColumns` C. `addNewColumns` D. `none`

Question 16. A data engineer creates a streaming query with a watermark of 15 minutes. The maximum event time observed is 10:45 AM. Which of the following events would be dropped as late data?

A. An event with timestamp 10:32 AM B. An event with timestamp 10:28 AM C. An event with timestamp 10:35 AM D. An event with timestamp 10:30 AM

Question 17. Which statement about Liquid Clustering is correct?

A. Liquid Clustering is specified using `OPTIMIZE ... ZORDER BY` B. Liquid Clustering is defined at table creation using `CLUSTER BY` and triggered by `OPTIMIZE` C. Liquid Clustering automatically partitions data by the specified columns D. Liquid Clustering requires manual file compaction after each write

Question 18. A data engineer registers an MLflow model in Unity Catalog. What is the correct URI format to load version 3 of the model?

A. `models:/analytics.ml_models.forecaster/3` B. `models://analytics.ml_models.forecaster@v3` C. `uc:/analytics.ml_models.forecaster/version/3` D. `registry:/analytics.ml_models.forecaster:3`

Question 19. A Delta Live Tables pipeline has the following table definitions:

```
@dlt.table
def bronze_events():
    return spark.readStream.format("cloudFiles")...

@dlt.table
def silver_events():
    return dlt.read_stream("bronze_events").filter(...)

@dlt.view
def gold_summary():
    return dlt.read("silver_events").groupBy(...).agg(...)
```

Which object is NOT persisted as a Delta table?

A. `bronze_events` B. `silver_events` C. `gold_summary` D. All three are persisted as Delta tables

Question 20. A data engineer needs to configure a Databricks Workflow with the following requirement: Task C should only run if both Task A AND Task B succeed. How should the dependency be configured?

A. Task C depends on Task A; Task B is independent B. Task C depends on both Task A and Task B (multiple dependencies) C. Task A depends on Task B; Task C depends on Task A D. All three tasks run in parallel

Question 21. What is the primary difference between `mergeSchema` and `overwriteSchema` options in Delta Lake writes?

A. `mergeSchema` is for append mode; `overwriteSchema` is for overwrite mode B. `mergeSchema` adds new columns to the existing schema; `overwriteSchema` completely replaces the schema C. `mergeSchema` works with SQL; `overwriteSchema` works with PySpark only D. They are equivalent and can be used interchangeably

Question 22. A company needs to comply with GDPR's "right to be forgotten." After deleting a customer's records from Delta tables, what additional step ensures the data is physically removed?

A. Run `RESTORE TABLE` to recreate the table without the deleted records B. Run `OPTIMIZE` to compact files and remove deleted records C. Run `VACUUM` to physically delete data files no longer referenced by the transaction log D. Drop and recreate the table

Question 23. Which feature of Azure Databricks allows you to restrict workspace access to specific IP address ranges?

A. VNet injection B. Private Link C. IP access lists D. Network Security Groups

Question 24. A data engineer uses the Feature Store to train a model with `create_training_set()` and Feature Lookups. What happens during batch inference using `score_batch()`?

A. The engineer must manually join feature tables before calling `score_batch()` B. The model automatically retrieves the latest features from the Feature Store using only primary key columns C. `score_batch()` requires all feature columns to be provided in the input DataFrame D. The Feature Store replays the training data for inference

Question 25. A Structured Streaming query reads from a Delta table source. The source table receives `UPDATE` and `DELETE` operations. What happens to the streaming query?

A. The query processes updates and deletes normally B. The query fails because streaming from Delta does not support updates/deletes by default C. The query ignores updates and deletes, processing only inserts D. The query automatically enables Change Data Feed

Question 26. Which SQL command shows the current permissions granted on a Unity Catalog table?

A. `DESCRIBE PERMISSIONS ON analytics.silver.orders;` B. `SHOW GRANTS ON TABLE analytics.silver.orders;` C. `SELECT * FROM information_schema.table_privileges WHERE table_name = 'orders';` D. `LIST ACL ON analytics.silver.orders ;`

Question 27. A data engineer needs to create a workspace-level cluster policy that requires all clusters to have auto-termination enabled with a maximum of 60 minutes. Which policy constraint type should be used?

A. `fixed` with value `60` B. `range` with `minValue: 1` and `maxValue: 60` C. `allowlist` with values `[30, 45, 60]` D. `unlimited`

Question 28. A data engineer has a Delta table with 1,000 small files (< 1 MB each). They run `OPTIMIZE`. After the operation, approximately how many files should the table have?

A. Still 1,000 files (OPTIMIZE does not change file count) B. 1 file (all data compacted into a single file) C. Approximately 1-10 files (compacted to target ~1 GB each, depending on total data size) D. 100 files (OPTIMIZE reduces file count by 10x)

Question 29. Which COPY INTO behavior differs from Auto Loader?

A. COPY INTO supports file format inference B. COPY INTO is a batch operation; Auto Loader is a streaming operation C. COPY INTO supports schema evolution D. COPY INTO can read from Kafka

Question 30. A data engineer queries `system.access.table_lineage`. What information does this system table provide?

A. Which users have permission to access each table B. Which tables were read by or written to by data operations, showing data flow C. The DDL history of table schema changes D. Storage statistics for each table

Question 31. A data engineer uses `mlflow.autolog()` in a notebook. They train a scikit-learn RandomForestClassifier. Which artifacts are automatically logged? (Select all that apply.)

A. Model hyperparameters B. Evaluation metrics (accuracy, F1, etc.) C. The trained model artifact D. The training dataset E. Feature importance plot

Question 32. A data engineer needs to enable Change Data Feed on an existing Delta table. Which command should they use?

A. `ALTER TABLE t SET TBLPROPERTIES ('delta.enableCDC' = 'true');` B. `ALTER TABLE t SET TBLPROPERTIES ('delta.enableChangeDataFeed' = 'true');` C. `ALTER TABLE t ENABLE CHANGE TRACKING;` D. `CREATE STREAM ON TABLE t;`

Question 33. A Databricks Workflow task fails with an OutOfMemory error. Which action is MOST likely to resolve the issue?

A. Increase the `max_retries` count B. Increase the cluster's driver or worker memory C. Change the task to run on a different schedule D. Add more tasks to the workflow to distribute the load

Question 34. A data engineer wants to create a Delta table where the data is physically stored in a specific ADLS Gen2 location rather than in the managed storage. What type of table should they create?

A. Managed table B. External table C. Temporary table D. Global temporary view

Question 35. Which Spark UI metric indicates data skew during a shuffle operation?

A. All tasks have approximately equal duration B. A few tasks take significantly longer than others with much larger input sizes C. The total shuffle write size is greater than 1 GB D. The number of tasks exceeds the number of partitions

Question 36. A data engineer creates a Workflow with three tasks: `extract`, `transform`, and `load`. The `transform` task depends on `extract`, and `load` depends on `transform`. The `extract` task fails. What happens?

A. `transform` and `load` are both skipped B. `transform` runs with empty input; `load` runs after `transform` C. `transform` is skipped; `load` runs anyway D. The entire workflow retries from `extract`

Question 37. A Delta table has `delta.autoOptimize.optimizeWrite` set to `true`. A write operation produces data that would naturally create 50 small files. What happens?

A. 50 files are written, then automatically compacted B. The write coalesces output into fewer, larger files before writing C. The write fails because optimizeWrite limits the number of files D. 50 files are written, and a background OPTIMIZE job is triggered

Question 38. A data engineer needs to create a SQL function that returns `true` if the current user is a member of a specific group. Which function should they use inside the SQL function definition?

A. `CURRENT_USER()` B. `IS_MEMBER('group_name')` C. `IS_ACCOUNT_GROUP_MEMBER('group_name')` D. `HAS_ROLE('group_name')`

Question 39. Which approach should a data engineer use to implement CI/CD for Databricks notebooks and job definitions?

A. Store notebooks in DBFS and use VACUUM for versioning B. Use Databricks Repos with Git integration and deploy with Databricks Asset Bundles or REST API C. Manually export and import notebooks between workspaces D. Use Delta Lake time travel to version notebooks

Question 40. A data engineer has a streaming pipeline that reads from Kafka and writes to Delta Lake. The pipeline must process data with at most 30-second latency. Which trigger configuration is most appropriate?

A. `trigger(availableNow=True)` B. `trigger(processingTime="30 seconds")` C. `trigger(once=True)` D. Default trigger (continuous micro-batches)

3.2 Practice Exam 2—Answer Key

Question 1: B. Databricks Workflows provide scheduling (including cron expressions), retry policies, email notifications, and multi-task dependencies. DLT is for pipeline definitions, not scheduling. Reference: Chapter 11.

Question 2: B. When a managed table is dropped, Unity Catalog deletes both the metadata and the underlying data files. External tables only remove the metadata, leaving data files intact. Reference: Chapter 3.

Question 3: B. `maxFilesPerTrigger` limits the number of new files processed from the source in each micro-batch. This is a rate-limiting mechanism to control processing volume. Reference: Chapter 9, Section 9.2.1.

Question 4: A. Without a filter on the partition column (`region`), Spark must scan all partitions. However, Delta Lake's data skipping (min/max statistics on `order_date`) may still help skip individual files within each partition. Reference: Chapter 4.

Question 5: B. Column masks are the correct approach for column-level security. A mask function returns the actual value for authorized groups and a masked value (like `NULL`) for others. Reference: Chapter 14, Section 14.4.2.

Question 6: C. The default minimum retention period for VACUUM is 168 hours (7 days). Setting a shorter period requires disabling the safety check with `delta.retentionDurationCheck.enabled = false`. Reference: Chapter 4, Section 4.7.3.

Question 7: A, B, D. Databricks AutoML supports classification, regression, and time-series forecasting. It does not support unsupervised learning tasks like clustering or anomaly detection. Reference: Chapter 13, Section 13.4.

Question 8: C. `expect_or_fail` causes the entire pipeline to fail immediately when a record violates the expectation. This is used for critical data quality rules that must never be violated. Reference: Chapter 10.

Question 9: B. Databricks redacts secret values in notebook output, displaying `[REDACTED]`. This prevents accidental exposure of secrets in shared notebooks or logs. Reference: Chapter 14, Section 14.5.

Question 10: B. `RESTORE TABLE ... TO VERSION AS OF` is the correct syntax for restoring a Delta table to a previous version. The RESTORE creates a new commit in the transaction log. Reference: Chapter 4, Section 4.6.4.

Question 11: A, B. Stream-stream joins require watermarks on both sides and a time constraint in the join condition. The streams can use different source types and do not need to share output modes. Reference: Chapter 9, Section 9.8.

Question 12: D. `DESCRIBE DETAIL` returns metadata about the table including format, location, number of files, size, partitioning, and table properties. It does not include query execution plans (use `EXPLAIN` for that). Reference: Chapter 4.

Question 13: B. `dbutils.jobs.taskValues` is the native Databricks mechanism for passing values between tasks in a Workflow. It is lightweight, typed, and designed for this purpose. Reference: Chapter 11.

Question 14: D. Both Single User and Shared modes enforce Unity Catalog permissions. Single User restricts the cluster to one user; Shared allows multiple users with UC ACLs enforced for each. No Isolation Shared does not enforce UC permissions. Reference: Chapter 14, Section 14.9.2.

Question 15: C. `schemaEvolutionMode = "addNewColumns"` automatically adds new columns from incoming files to the target table's schema. `rescue` places new columns in a rescue column. Reference: Chapter 6.

Question 16: B. Watermark threshold = 10:45 AM - 15 minutes = 10:30 AM. Events with timestamps strictly before 10:30 AM may be dropped. 10:28 AM is before 10:30 AM and would be dropped. 10:30 AM, 10:32 AM, and 10:35 AM are at or after the threshold. Reference: Chapter 9, Section 9.6.

Question 17: B. Liquid Clustering is defined at table creation using `CLUSTER BY` and is triggered when `OPTIMIZE` is run on the table. It replaces both Z-ORDER and traditional partitioning. Reference: Chapter 4, Section 4.7.4.

Question 18: A. The correct URI format for a specific model version is `models:/catalog.schema.model_name/version_number`. The `@` symbol is used for aliases, not version numbers. Reference: Chapter 13, Section 13.3.2.

Question 19: C. `dlt.view` creates a temporary view that is computed during pipeline execution but not persisted as a Delta table. It is useful for intermediate computations. `dlt.table` creates persisted Delta tables. Reference: Chapter 10.

Question 20: B. Databricks Workflows support multiple dependencies per task. Task C can be configured to depend on both Task A and Task B, and it will only run when both succeed. Reference: Chapter 11.

Question 21: B. `mergeSchema` adds new columns from the incoming data to the existing table schema while preserving existing columns. `overwriteSchema` completely replaces the table schema with the schema of the incoming data. Reference: Chapter 4, Section 4.8.

Question 22: C. VACUUM physically removes data files that are no longer referenced by the transaction log. After DELETE removes records logically, VACUUM is needed to ensure the old data files containing the deleted records are physically removed from storage. Reference: Chapter 14, Section 14.11.2.

Question 23: C. IP access lists restrict which IP addresses or CIDR ranges can access the Databricks workspace. VNet injection controls cluster network placement; Private Link controls connectivity to Azure services. Reference: Chapter 14, Section 14.6.3.

Question 24: B. When a model is trained with Feature Lookups, the lookup logic is packaged into the model. During `score_batch()`, the Feature Store automatically retrieves the latest features using only the primary key columns provided in the input DataFrame. Reference: Chapter 13, Section 13.5.6.

Question 25: B. By default, streaming reads from Delta tables do not support source tables that receive updates or deletes. The stream expects an append-only source. To handle changes, enable Change Data Feed and use `readChangeFeed = true`. Reference: Chapter 9, Section 9.11.

Question 26: B. `SHOW GRANTS ON TABLE` displays all current permission grants on a Unity Catalog table, including the grantee, permission type, and whether the grant was inherited. Reference: Chapter 14, Section 14.3.3.

Question 27: B. A `range` constraint with `minValue: 1` and `maxValue: 60` ensures auto-termination is always between 1 and 60 minutes. A `fixed` value would force exactly 60 minutes with no user choice. Reference: Chapter 14, Section 14.9.1.

Question 28: C. OPTIMIZE compacts small files into larger files targeting approximately 1 GB each. The resulting file count depends on total data size. For 1,000 small files with a small total size, the result might be 1-10 files. Reference: Chapter 4, Section 4.7.1.

Question 29: B. COPY INTO is a SQL-based batch operation that runs once per execution. Auto Loader is a streaming source that continuously monitors for new files. This is the fundamental architectural difference between the two ingestion methods. Reference: Chapter 6.

Question 30: B. `system.access.table_lineage` tracks the data flow between tables—which operations read from and wrote to which tables. This is used for understanding data dependencies and impact analysis. Reference: Chapter 14, Section 14.8.3.

Question 31: A, B, C, E. MLflow autologging for scikit-learn captures hyperparameters, evaluation metrics, the trained model artifact, and feature importance plots. The training dataset is NOT logged (it could be very large and contain sensitive data). Reference: Chapter 13, Section 13.2.3.

Question 32: B. The correct table property is `delta.enableChangeDataFeed`. The property name `delta.enableCDC` is not valid. `ENABLE CHANGE TRACKING` and `CREATE STREAM` are not valid Databricks commands. Reference: Chapter 9, Section 9.11.

Question 33: B. OutOfMemory errors are caused by insufficient memory for the workload. Increasing driver or worker memory (by selecting a larger instance type) is the most direct fix. Retries would just repeat the same failure. Reference: Chapter 12.

Question 34: B. External tables store data in a user-specified location (like ADLS Gen2) rather than in Unity Catalog's managed storage. The metadata is managed by Unity Catalog, but the data files remain at the specified external location. Reference: Chapter 3.

Question 35: B. Data skew is indicated when a small number of tasks in a stage take significantly longer than others and process much more data. This means the data is unevenly distributed across partitions. Reference: Chapter 12.

Question 36: A. When a task fails, all downstream dependent tasks are skipped. Since `transform` depends on `extract` (which failed), `transform` is skipped. Since `load` depends on `transform` (which was skipped), `load` is also skipped. Reference: Chapter 11.

Question 37: B. `optimizeWrite` coalesces small output partitions during the write operation itself, producing fewer, larger files. This is different from `autoCompact`, which runs a compaction after the write. Reference: Chapter 4, Section 4.10.

Question 38: C. `IS_ACCOUNT_GROUP_MEMBER('group_name')` is the Unity Catalog function for checking whether the current user belongs to a specific account-level group. This is used in row filter and column mask functions. Reference: Chapter 14, Section 14.4.

Question 39: B. Databricks Repos provides Git integration for version-controlling notebooks and code. Databricks Asset Bundles (DABs) or the REST API enable CI/CD deployment of jobs, notebooks, and configurations across workspaces. Reference: Chapter 11.

Question 40: B. `trigger(processingTime="30 seconds")` processes a micro-batch every 30 seconds, matching the latency requirement. The default trigger (continuous) would provide lower latency but use more resources. `availableNow` and `once` are batch-style triggers that stop after processing. Reference: Chapter 9, Section 9.5.

4

Practice Exam 3

4.1 Questions

Question 1. A data engineer needs to create a pipeline that reads CSV files from cloud storage, applies schema inference, handles schema changes automatically, and processes files incrementally. Which ingestion method is most appropriate?

A. `spark.read.csv()` in a batch job B. Auto Loader with `cloudFiles` format C. `COPY INTO` command D. `spark.readStream.format("csv")`

Question 2. A Unity Catalog catalog named `production` contains a schema named `finance` with a table named `revenue`. A user has `USAGE` on `production`, `USAGE` on `finance`, and `SELECT` on `revenue`. The user runs:

```
UPDATE production.finance.revenue SET amount = 0 WHERE region = 'test';
```

What happens?

A. The update succeeds B. The update fails because the user lacks `MODIFY` permission C. The update fails because the user lacks `UPDATE` permission D. The update fails because the user lacks `ALL PRIVILEGES`

Question 3. A data engineer needs to implement a slowly changing dimension (SCD Type 2) pattern. Which Delta Lake operation is best suited for this?

A. `UPDATE` B. `INSERT` C. `MERGE` D. `DELETE`

Question 4. Which of the following is a valid output mode for a Structured Streaming query that performs a `groupBy().count()` aggregation WITHOUT a watermark?

A. Append B. Complete C. Both Append and Complete D. Neither—a watermark is required for all aggregations

Question 5. A data engineer runs `OPTIMIZE` on a Delta table that uses Liquid Clustering with `CLUSTER BY (region, order_date)`. After optimization, which statement is true?

A. The table is partitioned into directories by `region` and `order_date` B. Data is co-located within files based on `region` and `order_date` values, enabling efficient data skipping C. Z-ORDER is automatically applied on `region` and `order_date` D. The table structure is unchanged; Liquid Clustering only affects reads

Question 6. A Databricks Workflow has a task with `max_retries = 2` and `min_retry_interval_millis = 60000`. The task fails on the first attempt, fails again on the first retry, and succeeds on the second retry. How many total attempts were made, and what was the minimum wait time?

A. 2 attempts, no wait time B. 3 attempts, minimum 60 seconds between retries C. 3 attempts, minimum 120 seconds total wait D. 4 attempts, minimum 60 seconds between retries

Question 7. A data engineer creates a Feature Store table and trains a model using Feature Lookups. During inference, the engineer only provides the `customer_id` column. How does the model access the features?

A. It cannot—all feature columns must be provided at inference time B. The Feature Store automatically looks up the latest feature values by `customer_id` C. The model uses cached feature values from training time D. The engineer must configure a separate feature serving endpoint

Question 8. Which Delta Lake table property controls how long transaction log entries are retained?

A. `delta.deletedFileRetentionDuration` B. `delta.logRetentionDuration` C. `delta.checkpointRetentionDuration` D. `delta.historyRetentionDuration`

Question 9. A data engineer needs to create an Azure Key Vault-backed secret scope. Which information is required? (Select all that apply.)

A. The Azure Key Vault resource ID B. The Key Vault DNS name C. The scope name D. The names of all secrets to be stored E. A personal access token for the Key Vault

Question 10. A Structured Streaming query uses session windows with a 10-minute gap:

```
result = (stream_df
    .withWatermark("event_time", "20 minutes")
    .groupBy(session_window("event_time", "10 minutes"), "user_id")
    .count())
```

Two events arrive for user 123: one at 10:00 AM and another at 10:08 AM. Do they belong to the same session?

A. Yes, because the gap between them (8 minutes) is less than the 10-minute session gap B. No, because each event creates its own session C. Yes, but only if the watermark has not passed D. No, because the watermark of 20 minutes exceeds the session gap

Question 11. A data engineer needs to configure a DLT pipeline to process data continuously with the lowest possible latency. Which pipeline mode should they use?

A. Triggered mode B. Continuous mode C. Scheduled mode D. Batch mode

Question 12. Which statement about Unity Catalog external tables is correct?

A. Dropping an external table deletes the underlying data files B. Dropping an external table removes only the metadata; data files remain C. External tables cannot be queried with Spark SQL D. External tables do not support Delta format

Question 13. A data engineer needs to implement a data quality check that logs a warning for any order with a negative amount but does NOT drop the record. Which DLT expectation should they use?

A. `@dlt.expect("positive_amount", "amount >= 0")` B. `@dlt.expect_or_drop("positive_amount", "amount >= 0")` C. `@dlt.expect_or_fail("positive_amount", "amount >= 0")` D. `@dlt.expect_or_warn("positive_amount", "amount >= 0")`

Question 14. A data engineer configures a streaming pipeline to write to a Delta table. Which option is mandatory for fault tolerance?

A. `outputMode` B. `checkpointLocation` C. `trigger` D. `queryName`

Question 15. A company has a prod workspace and a dev workspace sharing the same Unity Catalog metastore. A data engineer in the dev workspace needs to read a table in the `prod_data` catalog. What permissions are needed?

A. The engineer needs workspace admin access to the prod workspace B. The engineer needs `USAGE` on `prod_data` catalog and its schema, plus `SELECT` on the table C. Cross-workspace access is not possible, even with a shared metastore D. The engineer needs `ALL PRIVILEGES` on the metastore

Question 16. A data engineer monitors a streaming query and notices that `stateOperator.numRowsTotal` is growing continuously. What is the most likely solution?

A. Increase the trigger interval B. Add or adjust a watermark to allow Spark to prune old state C. Switch from append to complete output mode D. Increase the cluster's memory

Question 17. Which of the following correctly describes the relationship between `OPTIMIZE` and `VACUUM` for a Delta table?

A. OPTIMIZE and VACUUM perform the same operation B. OPTIMIZE compacts small files into larger ones; VACUUM removes old data files no longer referenced by the log C. VACUUM compacts files; OPTIMIZE removes old files D. Both must be run together in a single command

Question 18. A data engineer creates a materialized view in a Delta Live Tables pipeline. When does the view's data get recomputed?

A. Every time the view is queried B. Only when the pipeline is run (triggered or scheduled) C. Continuously in real-time D. Once during pipeline creation, then never again

Question 19. A data engineer needs to implement encryption at rest using customer-managed keys (CMK) for their Databricks workspace. Where should the encryption key be stored?

A. In a Databricks secret scope B. In Azure Key Vault C. In the workspace's DBFS root D. In an environment variable on the cluster

Question 20. A data engineer creates a Spark SQL UDF:

```
CREATE FUNCTION analytics.transforms.clean_phone(phone STRING)
RETURNS STRING
RETURN regexp_replace(phone, '[^0-9]', '');
```

Who can execute this function?

A. Any user in the workspace B. Any user with `USAGE` on the `analytics` catalog and `transforms` schema, plus `EXECUTE` on the function C. Only the function creator D. Only users with `ALL PRIVILEGES` on the catalog

Question 21. A streaming pipeline uses `trigger(processingTime="1 minute")`. If a micro-batch takes 90 seconds to process, what happens?

A. The next micro-batch starts immediately after the current one finishes B. The pipeline fails because the trigger interval was exceeded C. The pipeline waits an additional 60 seconds after the current batch completes D. The pipeline drops data that arrived during the extra 30 seconds

Question 22. A data engineer needs to create a table that includes a constraint ensuring the `status` column only contains values 'active', 'inactive', or 'pending'. Which constraint type should they use?

A. NOT NULL constraint B. CHECK constraint C. UNIQUE constraint D. FOREIGN KEY constraint

Question 23. In the context of MLflow on Databricks, what is the purpose of model aliases like "champion" and "challenger"?

A. They automatically trigger A/B testing in model serving endpoints B. They are flexible labels assigned to specific model versions to designate their purpose in the lifecycle C. They are required stages that every model must pass through before deployment D. They determine the compute resources allocated to model serving

Question 24. A data engineer runs the following:

```
df.write.format("delta") \
    .mode("overwrite") \
    .option("overwriteSchema", "true") \
    .saveAsTable("analytics.silver.customers")
```

What is the effect of `overwriteSchema = true`?

A. Only the schema is overwritten; the data remains unchanged B. Both the data and the schema of the table are completely replaced C. The schema is merged with new columns added D. The operation fails because you cannot overwrite the schema of an existing table

Question 25. A data engineer needs to monitor the cost of Databricks compute resources. Which system table provides billing and usage information?

A. `system.access.audit` B. `system.billing.usage` C. `system.compute.clusters` D. `system.billing.list_prices`

Question 26. A data engineer is designing a medallion architecture. Which layer typically contains raw, unvalidated data in its original format?

A. Gold layer B. Silver layer C. Bronze layer D. Platinum layer

Question 27. A data engineer creates a streaming query that reads from a Kafka topic. The query writes to a Delta table with `outputMode("append")`. After running for 24 hours, the query is stopped and restarted. From which point does the query resume?

A. From the beginning of the Kafka topic B. From the latest offset in the Kafka topic C. From the last committed offset recorded in the checkpoint D. From the offset specified in `startingOffsets`

Question 28. Which command should a data engineer use to see the physical location, size, and number of files of a Delta table?

A. `DESCRIBE TABLE analytics.silver.orders;` B. `DESCRIBE EXTENDED analytics.silver.orders;` C. `DESCRIBE DETAIL analytics.silver.orders;` D. `SHOW TABLE PROPERTIES analytics.silver.orders;`

Question 29. A data engineer configures Private Link for their Databricks workspace. Which type of Private Link connection ensures that cluster-to-control-plane communication stays on the Azure private network?

A. Front-end Private Link B. Back-end Private Link C. Storage Private Link D. Identity Private Link

Question 30. A data engineer creates a Delta table with the following:

```
ALTER TABLE analytics.silver.orders
ADD CONSTRAINT valid_amount CHECK (amount > 0);
```

An existing row in the table has `amount = -10`. What happens?

A. The constraint is not created because existing data violates it B. The constraint is created but only applies to future inserts/updates C. The existing row is automatically deleted D. The existing row is updated to `amount = 0`

Question 31. A data engineer needs to query the MLflow experiment results to find the run with the lowest RMSE. Which function should they use?

A. `mlflow.get_best_run()` B. `mlflow.search_runs()` with `order_by=["metrics.rmse ASC"]` C. `mlflow.list_runs(sort_by="rmse")` D. `mlflow.experiments.get_top_run(metric="rmse")`

Question 32. Which Delta Lake feature allows a streaming consumer to see both the old and new values for updated rows?

A. Time travel B. Transaction log C. Change Data Feed D. Delta Sharing

Question 33. A data engineer creates an Auto Loader pipeline that schema-infers columns from JSON files. A new file arrives with an additional field `loyalty_tier` that was not in previous files. If `schemaEvolutionMode` is set to `rescue`, what happens?

A. The pipeline fails with a schema mismatch error B. The `loyalty_tier` values are placed in a `_rescued_data` column as JSON C. The `loyalty_tier` column is automatically added to the schema D. The `loyalty_tier` field is silently dropped

Question 34. A data engineer sets up a Databricks Workflow with an email notification configured for "On Failure." The workflow has three tasks. Task 2 fails, but Tasks 1 and 3 succeed. When is the email notification sent?

A. Immediately when Task 2 fails B. After the entire workflow completes (since the workflow overall failed) C. No email is sent because Task 3 succeeded D. Three emails are sent, one for each task

Question 35. Which statement about Unity Catalog Volumes is correct?

A. Volumes can only store Delta format files B. Volumes provide governed access to non-tabular files like CSVs, images, and model artifacts C. Volumes replace external locations for all use cases D. Volumes are only accessible from Python, not SQL

Question 36. A data engineer needs to implement a daily job that scores 10 million customer records using a registered MLflow model. Which approach is most efficient?

A. Deploy the model to a serving endpoint and send 10 million API requests B. Use `mlflow.pyfunc.spark_udf()` to create a Spark UDF and apply it to the customer DataFrame C. Load the model with `mlflow.pyfunc.load_model()` and iterate through records with a for loop D. Use AutoML to retrain the model on the 10 million records

Question 37. A data engineer creates a streaming table in Delta Live Tables. The source is Auto Loader reading from cloud storage. If the pipeline is stopped and restarted, what happens?

A. All files are reprocessed from the beginning B. Only new files since the last pipeline run are processed C. The pipeline fails because the checkpoint was lost D. The pipeline starts processing from the latest file only

Question 38. Which command displays the data lineage for a Unity Catalog table, showing upstream and downstream dependencies?

A. `DESCRIBE LINEAGE analytics.silver.orders;` B. Query `system.access.table_lineage` filtering on the table name C. `SHOW DEPENDENCIES analytics.silver.orders;` D. `DESCRIBE HISTORY analytics.silver.orders;`

Question 39. A data engineer configures a cluster policy with the following JSON:

```
{
    "spark_version": {
        "type": "fixed",
        "value": "15.0.x-scala2.12"
    }
}
```

What effect does this have?

A. Users must select version "15.0.x-scala2.12" from a dropdown B. Users cannot change the Spark version—it is automatically set to "15.0.x-scala2.12" C. Users can choose any version starting with "15.0" D. The policy has no effect; `spark_version` cannot be constrained

Question 40. A data engineer has a Delta table where queries frequently filter on `customer_id` and `order_date`. The table currently has no optimization. The table has 500 GB of data. Which optimization strategy should the engineer implement?

A. Partition by `customer_id` and Z-ORDER by `order_date` B. Use Liquid Clustering with `CLUSTER BY (customer_id , order_date)` C. Partition by `order_date` only D. Z-ORDER by `customer_id` only

---

4.2 Practice Exam 3—Answer Key

Question 1: B. Auto Loader (`cloudFiles` format) provides incremental file processing, automatic schema inference, schema evolution handling, and exactly-once semantics. Batch `spark.read` does not process incrementally. `COPY INTO` does not handle schema evolution as flexibly. Reference: Chapter 6.

Question 2: B. `UPDATE` is a DML operation that requires `MODIFY` permission in Unity Catalog. `SELECT` only grants read access. There is no separate `UPDATE` permission – `MODIFY` covers INSERT, UPDATE, and DELETE. Reference: Chapter 14, Section 14.3.2.

Question 3: C. MERGE is ideal for SCD Type 2 because it can match on business keys, close existing records (update end date), and insert new records, all in a single atomic operation. Reference: Chapter 4, Section 4.5.3.

Question 4: B. Without a watermark, aggregation queries support Complete and Update output modes only. Append mode requires a watermark for aggregations because the system must know when to finalize results. Reference: Chapter 9, Section 9.4.

Question 5: B. Liquid Clustering co-locates data within files based on the clustering columns, enabling efficient data skipping. Unlike traditional partitioning, it does not create separate directories. It is a distinct mechanism from Z-ORDER. Reference: Chapter 4, Section 4.7.4.

Question 6: B. The initial attempt (1) plus two retries (2 + 3) equals 3 total attempts. `min_retry_interval_millis = 60000` means at least 60 seconds between each retry attempt. Reference: Chapter 11.

Question 7: B. When a model is trained with Feature Lookups, the lookup logic is packaged into the model. During inference, the Feature Store automatically retrieves the latest features by primary key. Reference: Chapter 13, Section 13.5.6.

Question 8: B. `delta.logRetentionDuration` controls how long transaction log entries (JSON commit files) are retained. Default is 30 days. `delta.deletedFileRetentionDuration` controls VACUUM retention for data files. Reference: Chapter 4, Section 4.10.

Question 9: A, B, C. Creating an Azure Key Vault-backed secret scope requires the Key Vault resource ID, the DNS name, and a name for the scope. You do not need to pre-specify secret names (they are resolved at access time), and authentication uses Azure AD, not PATs. Reference: Chapter 14, Section 14.5.2.

Question 10: A. Session windows group events by activity. Two events from the same user within the 10-minute gap threshold belong to the same session. The 8-minute gap between 10:00 and 10:08 is less than 10 minutes, so they are in the same session. Reference: Chapter 9, Section 9.7.3.

Question 11: B. DLT continuous mode processes data with the lowest possible latency by running micro-batches as fast as possible, similar to the default Structured Streaming trigger. Triggered mode runs once per pipeline trigger. Reference: Chapter 10.

Question 12: B. Dropping an external table removes only the Unity Catalog metadata. The underlying data files in cloud storage are not affected. This is the key difference between external and managed tables. Reference: Chapter 3.

Question 13: A. `@dlt.expect` logs a warning when records violate the expectation but does not drop them. `expect_or_drop` drops violating records. `expect_or_fail` fails the pipeline. There is no `expect_or_warn` decorator. Reference: Chapter 10.

Question 14: B. `checkpointLocation` is mandatory for production streaming queries. It stores offsets, state, and commit information needed for exactly-once processing and fault recovery. Reference: Chapter 9, Section 9.9.

Question 15: B. When workspaces share a metastore, cross-workspace data access is governed by Unity Catalog permissions. The engineer needs the standard permission chain: `USAGE` on catalog and schema, plus `SELECT` on the table. No workspace admin access is needed. Reference: Chapter 3 and Chapter 14.

Question 16: B. Unbounded state growth is caused by the absence of a watermark. Without a watermark, Spark cannot determine when aggregation groups are finalized and must retain all state indefinitely. Adding a watermark allows Spark to prune state for groups past the threshold. Reference: Chapter 9, Section 9.6.

Question 17: B. OPTIMIZE compacts small files into larger, more efficient files. VACUUM physically removes old data files that are no longer referenced by the current transaction log state. They are complementary operations, not alternatives. Reference: Chapter 4, Section 4.7.

Question 18: B. Materialized views in DLT are recomputed when the pipeline runs. They perform a full recomputation of the view's query, ensuring the results reflect the latest source data. They are not continuously updated or recomputed on every query. Reference: Chapter 10.

Question 19: B. Customer-managed encryption keys for Azure Databricks must be stored in Azure Key Vault. The workspace is configured to reference the Key Vault URI, key name, and key version for encryption operations. Reference: Chapter 14, Section 14.7.2.

Question 20: B. SQL UDFs in Unity Catalog follow the standard permission model. Users need `USAGE` on the parent catalog and schema, plus `EXECUTE` on the function itself. Reference: Chapter 14, Section 14.3.2.

Question 21: A. If a micro-batch takes longer than the trigger interval, the next micro-batch starts immediately after the current one finishes. Structured Streaming does not fail or drop data—it simply falls behind and catches up when possible. Reference: Chapter 9, Section 9.5.

Question 22: B. A CHECK constraint validates that column values satisfy a boolean expression: `CHECK (status IN ('active', 'inactive', 'pending'))`. Delta Lake supports CHECK and NOT NULL constraints. UNIQUE and FOREIGN KEY constraints are not supported. Reference: Chapter 4, Section 4.9.1.

Question 23: B. Aliases in the Unity Catalog model registry are flexible string labels (like "champion" or "challenger") that can be assigned to any model version. They replace the legacy fixed stages (Staging, Production, Archived) and are more flexible. They do not automatically configure serving endpoints. Reference: Chapter 13, Section 13.3.2.

Question 24: B. With `mode("overwrite")` and `overwriteSchema = true`, both the data and the schema of the table are completely replaced. This is a destructive operation that replaces the entire table definition. `mergeSchema` is the non-destructive alternative that adds new columns. Reference: Chapter 4, Section 4.8.

Question 25: B. `system.billing.usage` provides detailed billing and compute usage information including DBU consumption, cluster runtime, and associated costs. Reference: Chapter 12.

Question 26: C. The bronze layer (also called the raw layer) contains data in its original, unvalidated format. The silver layer contains cleaned and validated data. The gold layer contains business-aggregated, consumption-ready data. Reference: Chapter 5.

Question 27: C. When a streaming query restarts, it reads the last committed offset from the checkpoint and resumes from that point. This is how exactly-once processing is guaranteed across restarts. `startingOffsets` is only used when there is no existing checkpoint. Reference: Chapter 9, Section 9.9.

Question 28: C. `DESCRIBE DETAIL` returns physical metadata about a Delta table including location, format, size, number of files, partitioning, and creation time. `DESCRIBE EXTENDED` shows schema and properties but not physical file details. Reference: Chapter 4.

Question 29: B. Back-end Private Link ensures that communication between the cluster (in the customer's VNet) and the Databricks control plane stays on the Azure private network. Front-end Private Link secures user (browser) access to the workspace. Reference: Chapter 14, Section 14.6.2.

Question 30: B. CHECK constraints in Delta Lake are only enforced on future writes (INSERT, UPDATE, MERGE). Existing data that violates the constraint is not affected when the constraint is added. The constraint is successfully created regardless of existing data. Reference: Chapter 4, Section 4.9.1.

Question 31: B. `mlflow.search_runs()` allows querying experiment runs with filters and ordering. Using `order_by=["metrics.rmse ASC"]` returns runs sorted by RMSE in ascending order, with the best (lowest) RMSE first. Reference: Chapter 13, Section 13.2.4.

Question 32: C. Change Data Feed (CDF) captures row-level changes including `update_preimage` (old values) and `update_postimage` (new values) for updated rows. Time travel shows full table snapshots, not individual row changes. Reference: Chapter 9, Section 9.11.

Question 33: B. When `schemaEvolutionMode = "rescue"`, columns not present in the inferred schema are placed as JSON in a `_rescued_data` column rather than failing or being dropped. This preserves the data without modifying the schema. Reference: Chapter 6.

Question 34: B. Workflow-level "On Failure" notifications are sent when the overall workflow status is failed. The notification is sent after the entire workflow completes, not when individual tasks fail. Since Task 2 failed, the workflow is marked as failed. Reference: Chapter 11.

Question 35: B. Unity Catalog Volumes provide governed access to non-tabular files such as CSVs, images, model artifacts, and other unstructured data. Volumes can store any file type and are accessible from both SQL and Python. Reference: Chapter 3.

Question 36: B. `mlflow.pyfunc.spark_udf()` creates a distributed Spark UDF from the model, enabling parallel scoring across the cluster. API calls for 10 million records would be extremely slow and expensive. A for loop would not leverage Spark's distributed processing. Reference: Chapter 13, Section 13.7.

Question 37: B. DLT streaming tables maintain checkpoint state between pipeline runs. When the pipeline restarts, Auto Loader resumes from where it left off, processing only new files. Reference: Chapter 10.

Question 38: B. `system.access.table_lineage` is the system table that tracks data lineage—which operations read from and wrote to which tables. There is no `DESCRIBE LINEAGE` or `SHOW DEPENDENCIES` command. `DESCRIBE HISTORY` shows DML operation history, not lineage. Reference: Chapter 14, Section 14.8.3.

Question 39: B. A `fixed` constraint means the value is automatically set and cannot be changed by the user. The user does not see a dropdown—the field is locked to the specified value. Reference: Chapter 14, Section 14.9.1.

Question 40: B. For a 500 GB table with frequent filters on two columns, Liquid Clustering (`CLUSTER BY`) is the recommended modern approach. It replaces both partitioning and Z-ORDER, adapts incrementally, and does not require upfront partitioning decisions. Partitioning by `customer_id` would create too many partitions (high cardinality). Reference: Chapter 4, Section 4.7.4.

4.3 Scoring Guide

Score	Assessment	Recommendation
90-100%	Excellent—You are well-prepared for the exam	Review any missed questions, then schedule the exam
80-89%	Good—Minor gaps in knowledge	Focus study on missed topics for 2-3 days, then retake
70-79%	Passing—But with some risk	Spend a week reviewing weak areas before the real exam
60-69%	Below passing—Significant gaps	Review the relevant chapters thoroughly and retake in 2 weeks
Below 60%	Not ready—Foundational gaps	Complete a full review of all chapters before attempting again

Remember that the real DP-750 exam may include question types not represented here, such as drag-and-drop ordering, case studies with multiple questions, and "select all that apply" with more than two correct answers. Practice these formats using Microsoft's official practice assessment if available.

4.4 Final Study Tips

1. **Focus on Delta Lake and Unity Catalog**—These are the two most heavily tested topics across all four exam domains.
2. **Understand the "why," not just the "how"**—The exam often asks which approach is *best* for a given scenario, requiring you to understand trade-offs.
3. **Know the permission chain**—`USAGE` on catalog □ `USAGE` on schema □ specific permission on object. This pattern appears in many questions.
4. **Practice with real code**—Run the code examples from this guide in a Databricks workspace. The exam tests practical understanding.
5. **Review streaming fundamentals**—Output modes, trigger types, watermarks, and checkpoints are tested repeatedly.
6. **Security is worth 15-20%**—Do not neglect Chapter 14. Questions about row filters, column masks, secret scopes, and network security are straightforward if you have studied them.
7. **Read every answer option**—Many exam questions have plausible-sounding wrong answers. Eliminate clearly wrong options first, then carefully compare the remaining choices.

Good luck on your DP-750 exam.

www.ingramcontent.com/pod-product-compliance
Lightning Source LLC
LaVergne TN
LVHW070910210926
848482LV00017B/1039